Poze cu bikini

Taylor Timms

Poze cu bikini
Taylor Timms

ISBN 978-0-9866426-6-1

Imprimat în USA sau UK

Free Online Seduction Course

As a thank you for buying this book, I would like to give you access to my online seduction course.

To claim your free spot, please go to
www.foreverlaid.com
and enter your valid email address now.

Also by Taylor Timms

Forever Laid Formula
Best Ways To Get Women To Sleep With You
ISBN 978-0-9866004-2-5

Best Gift Ideas For Women
Perfect Gifts Ideas For Any Special Occasion
ISBN 978-0-9866004-4-9

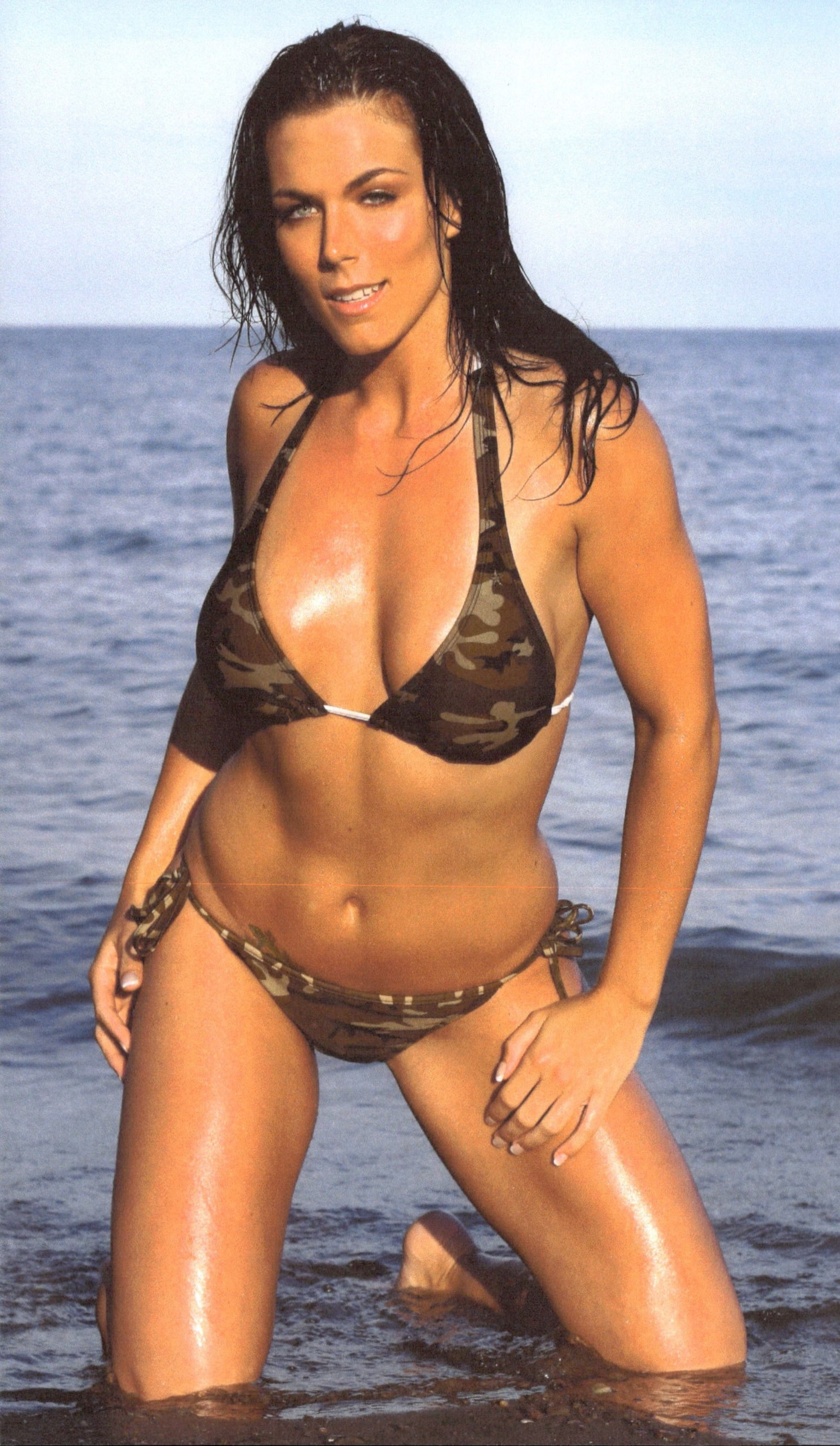

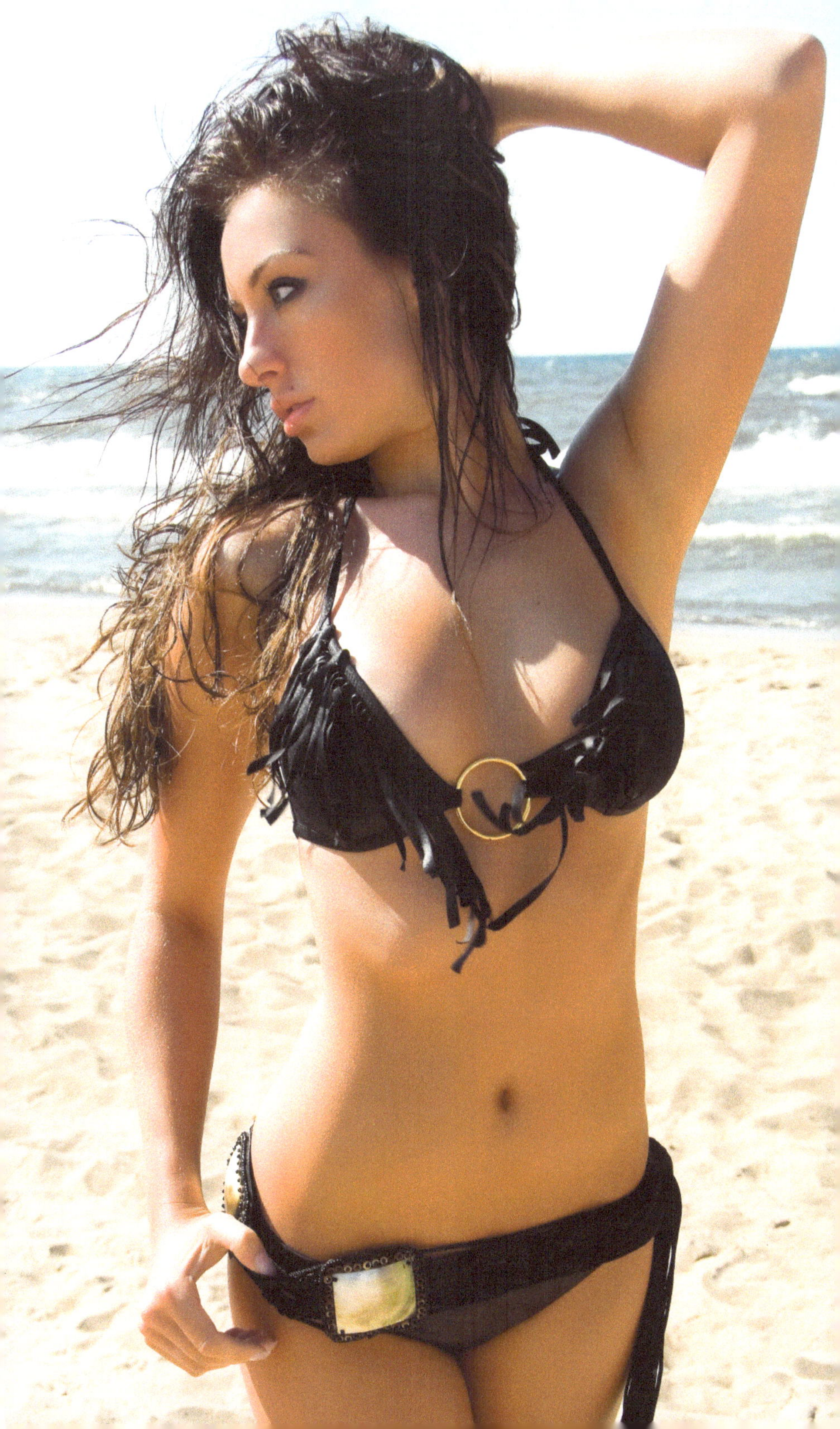

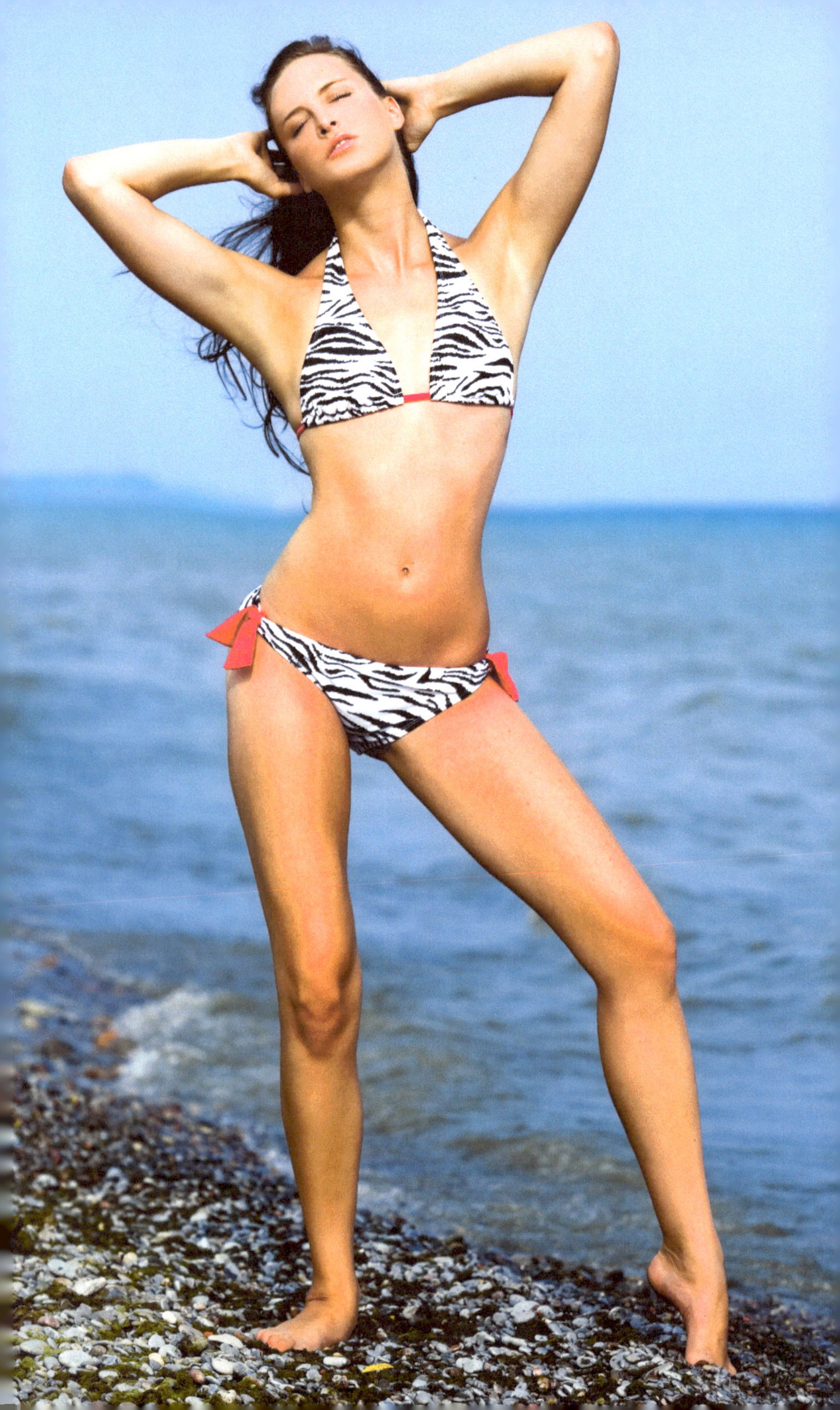

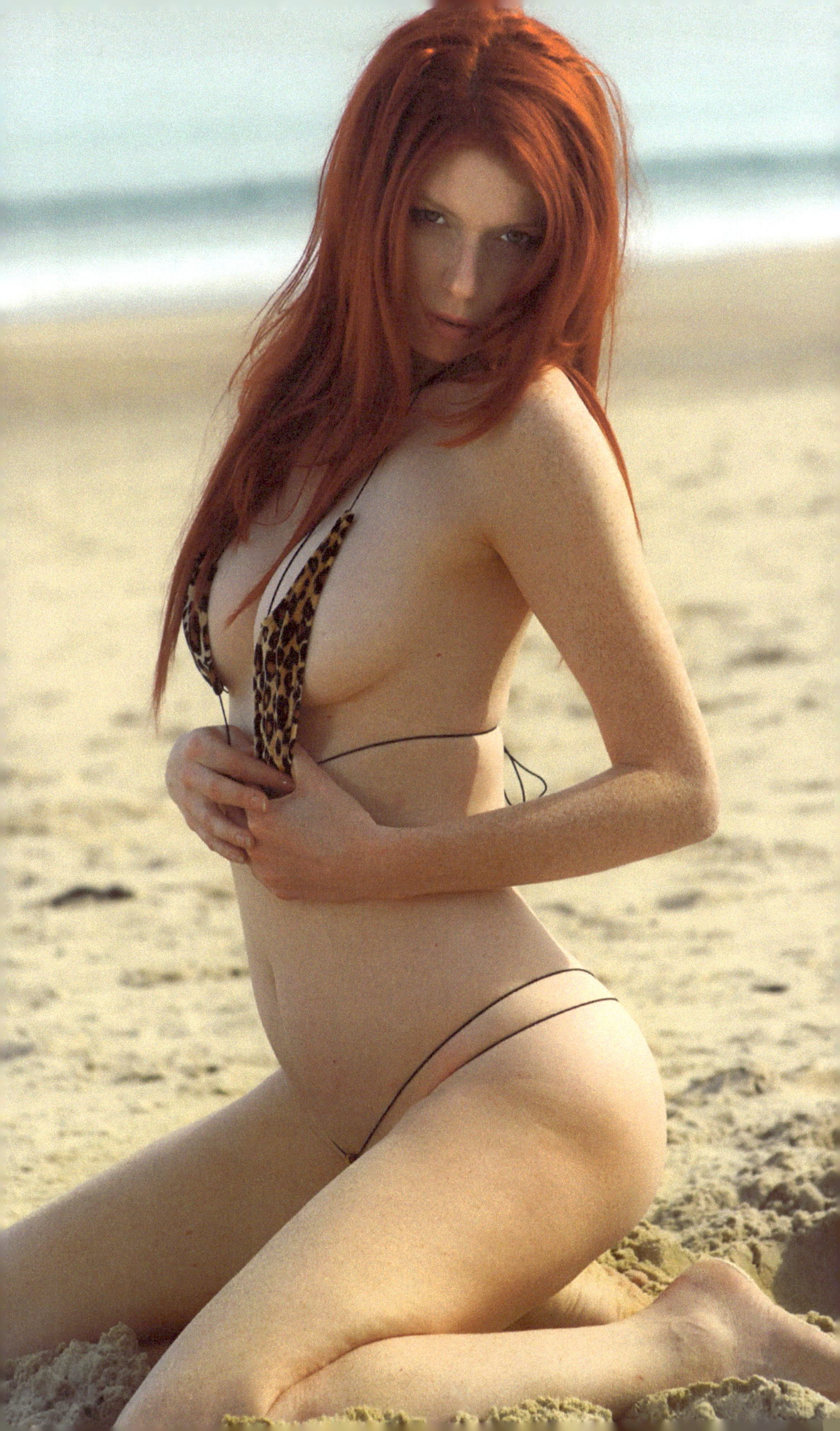

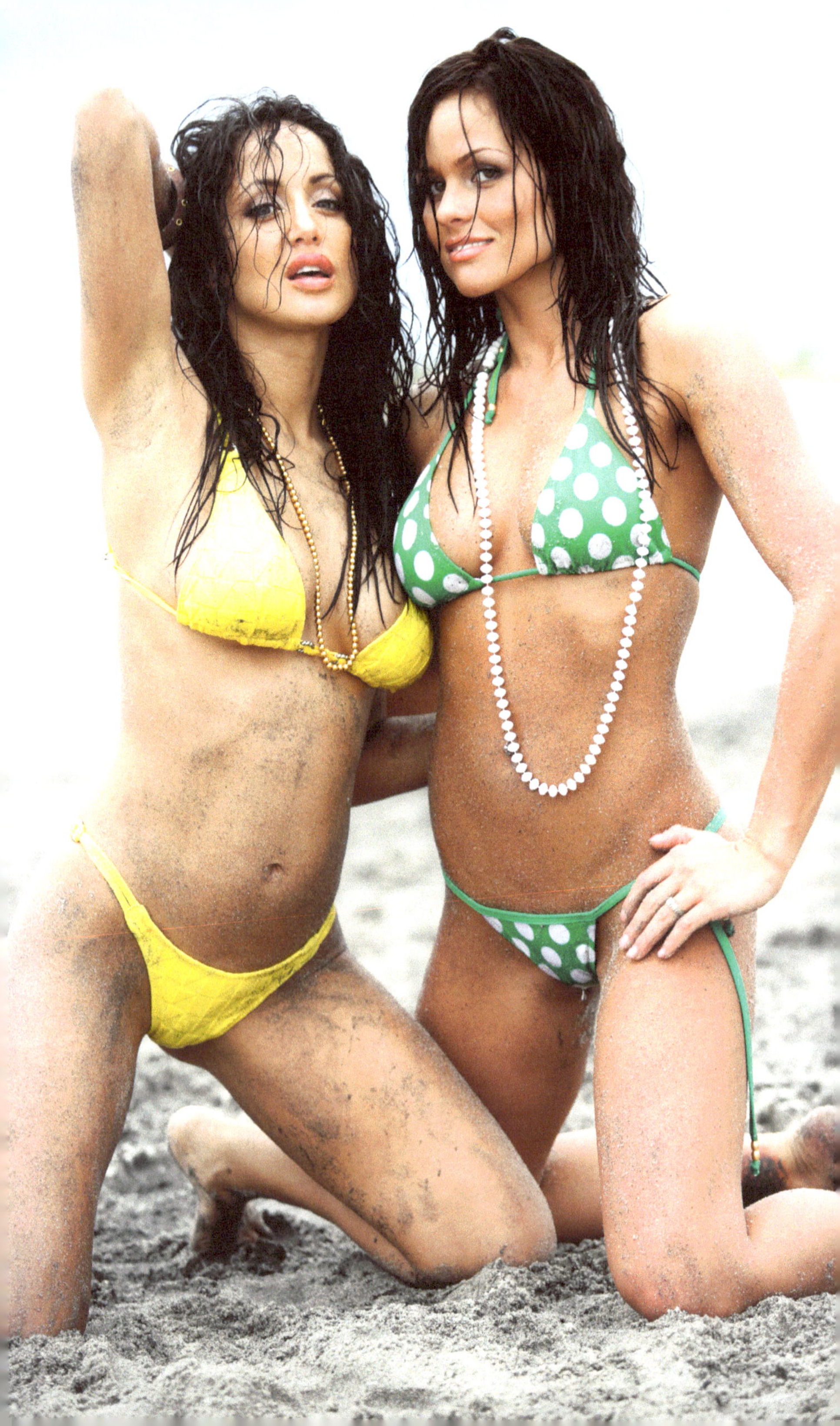

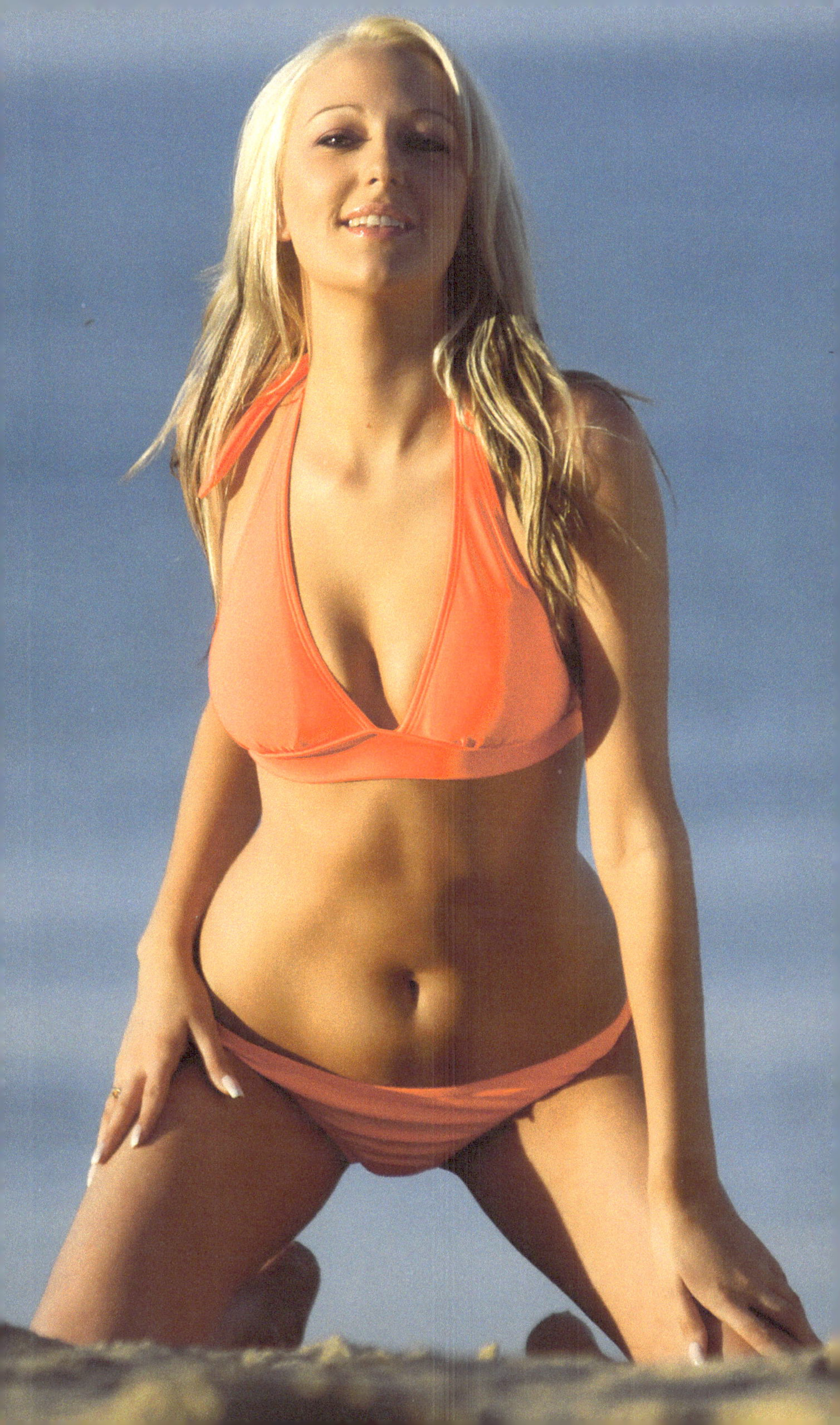

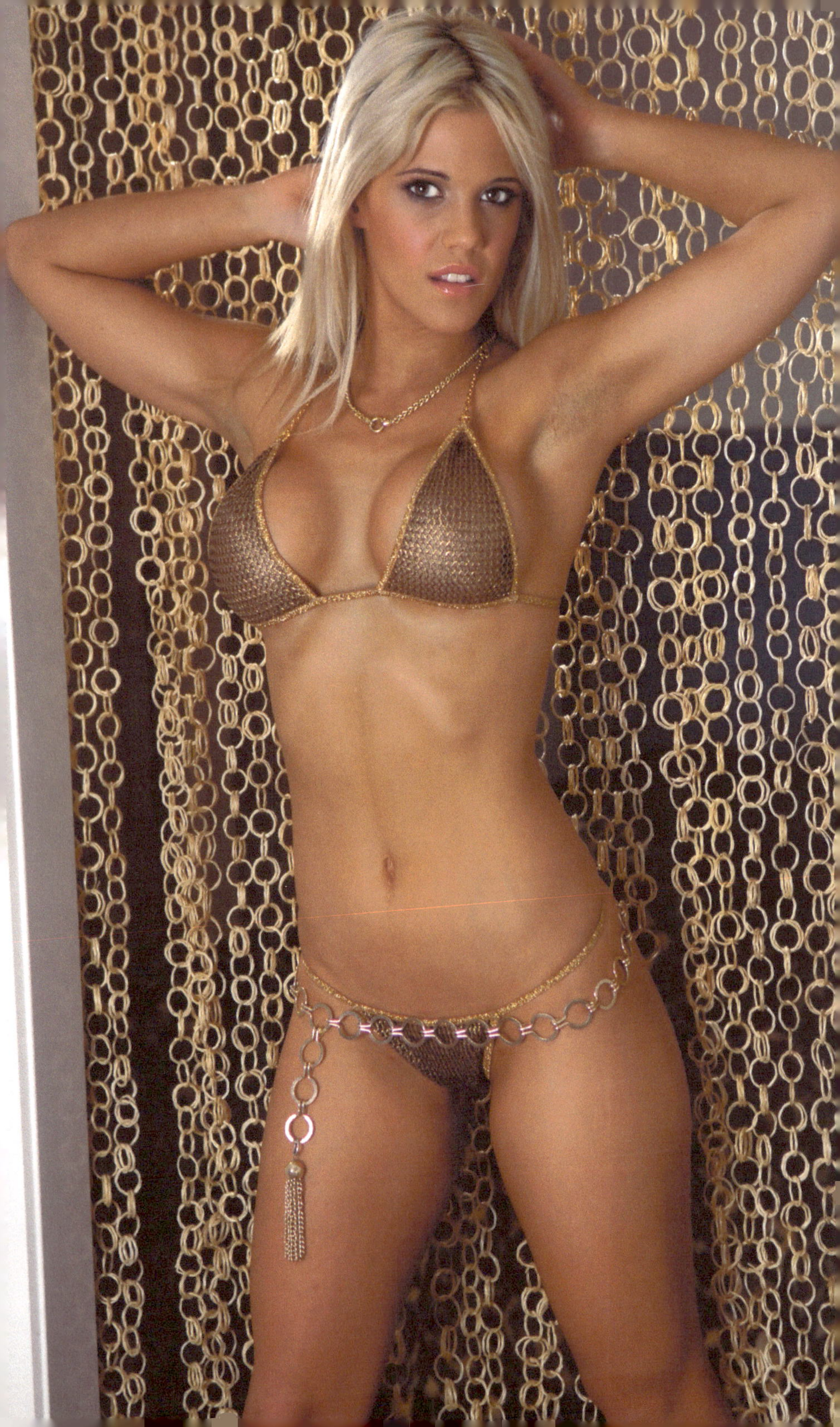

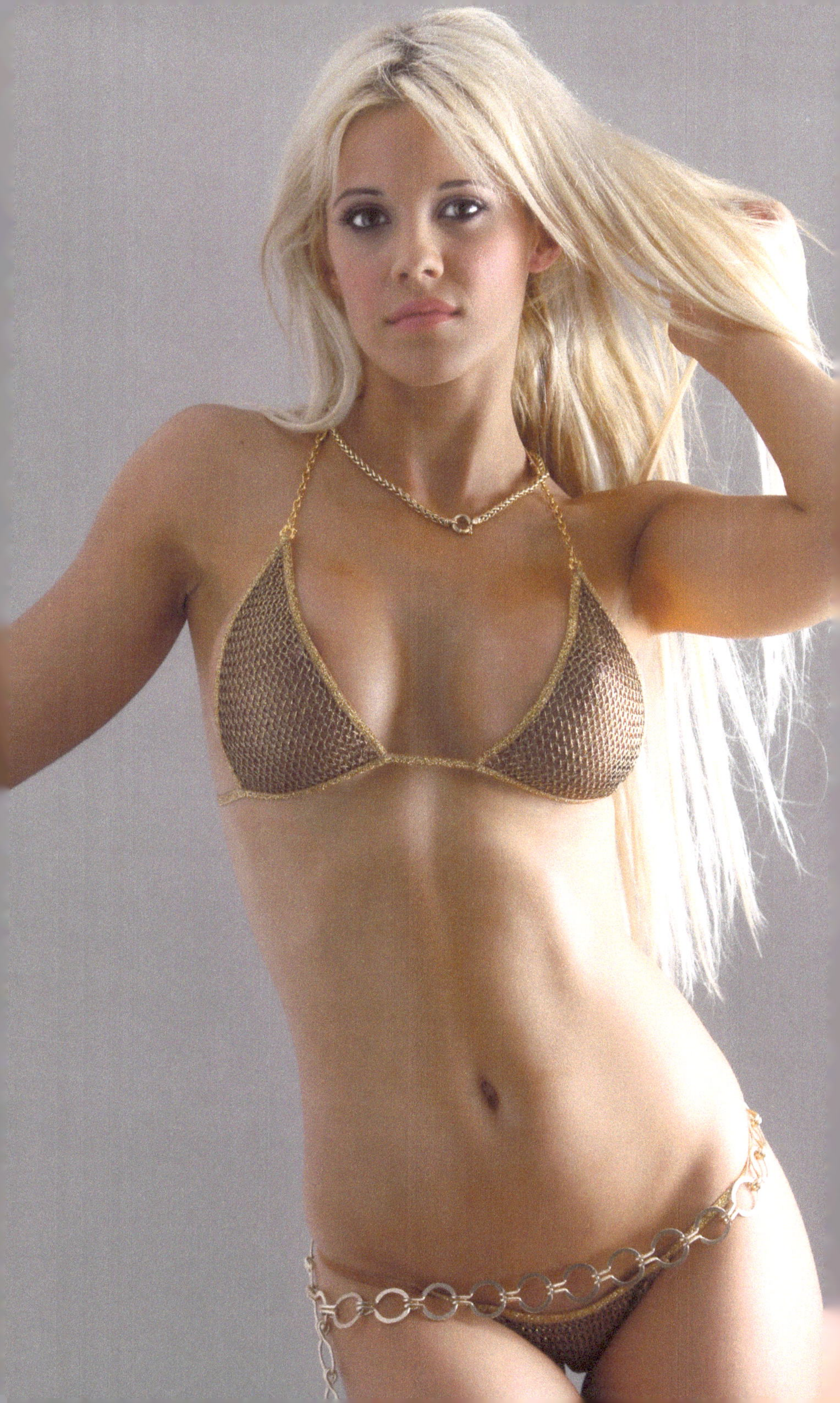

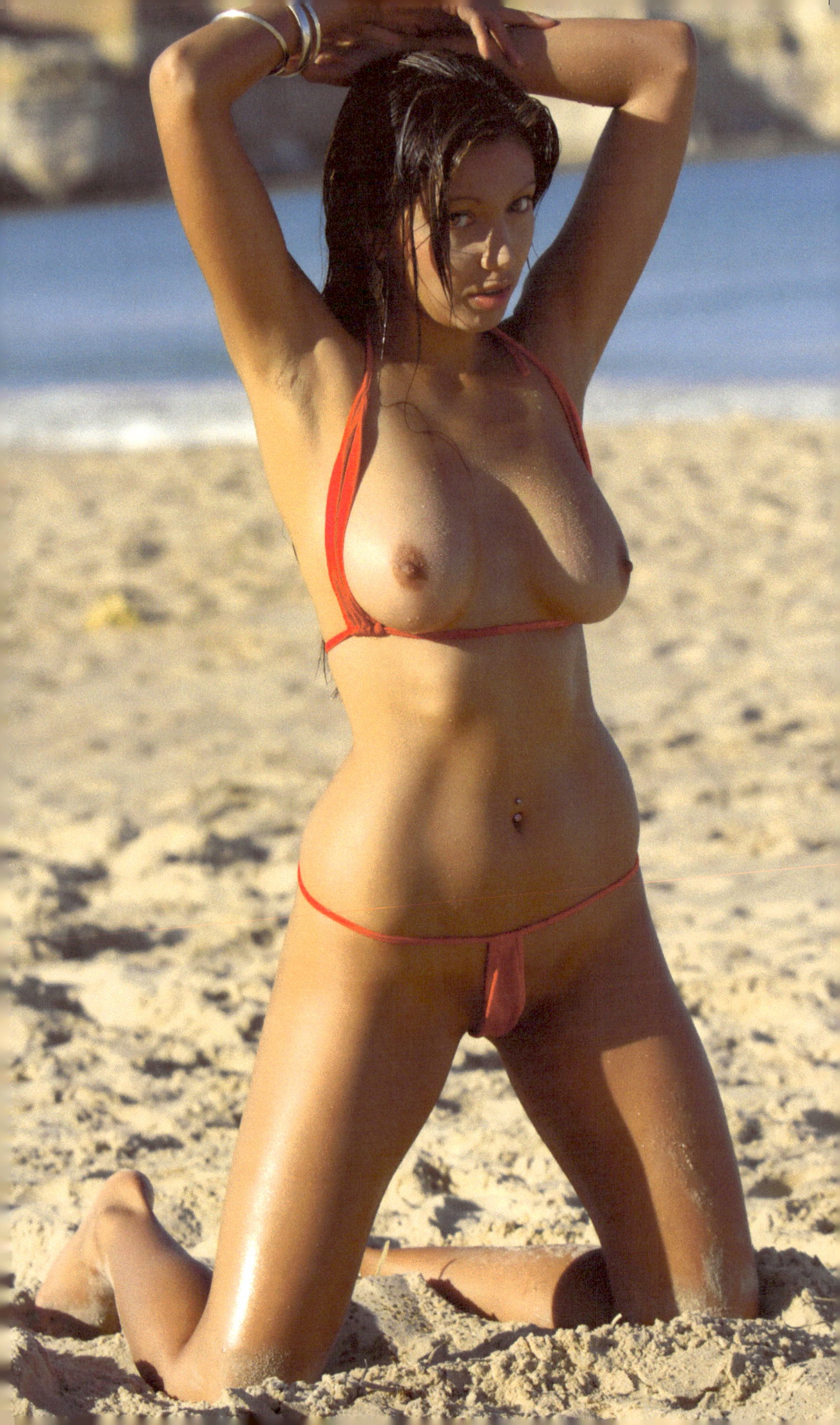

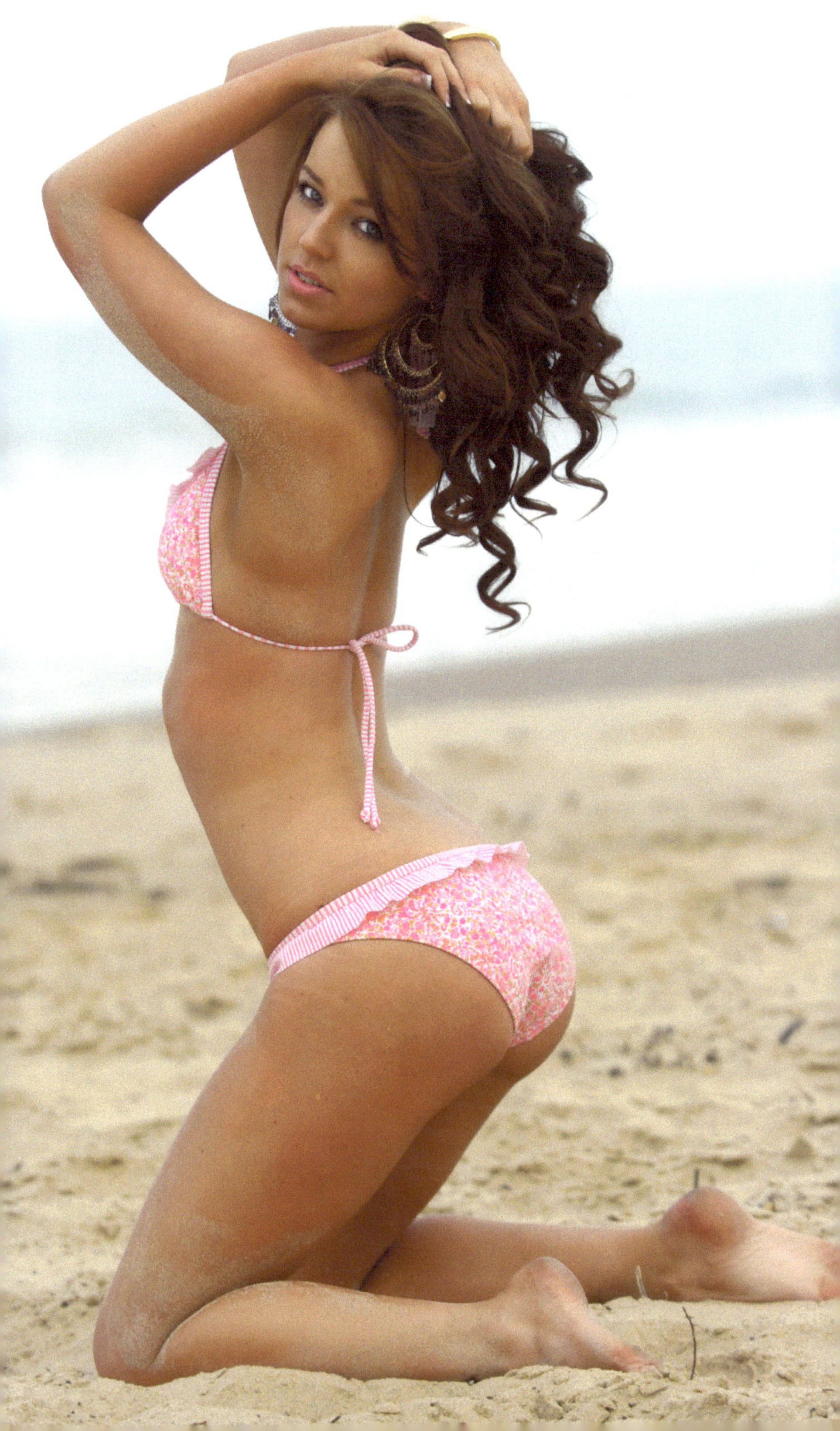

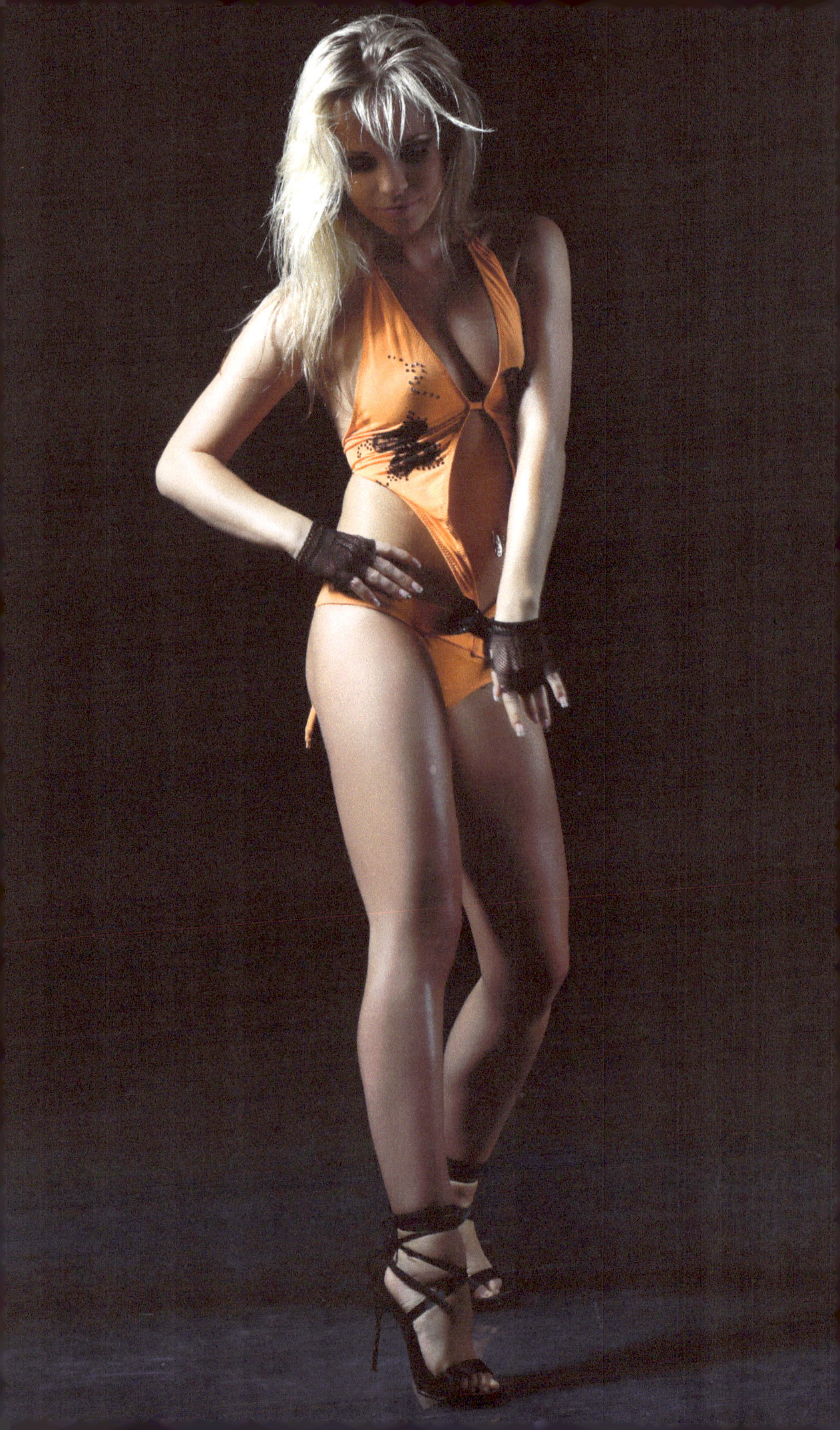

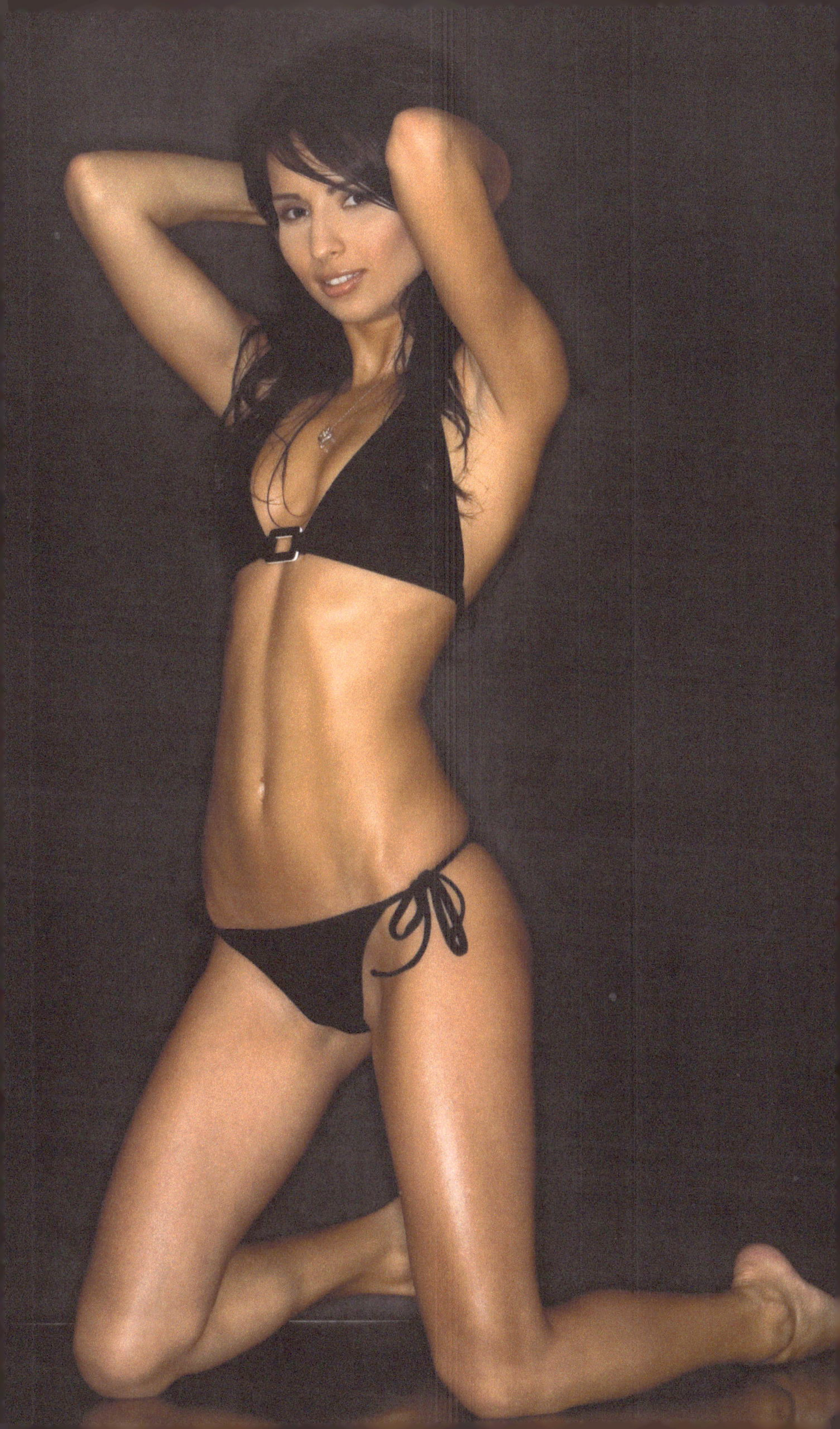

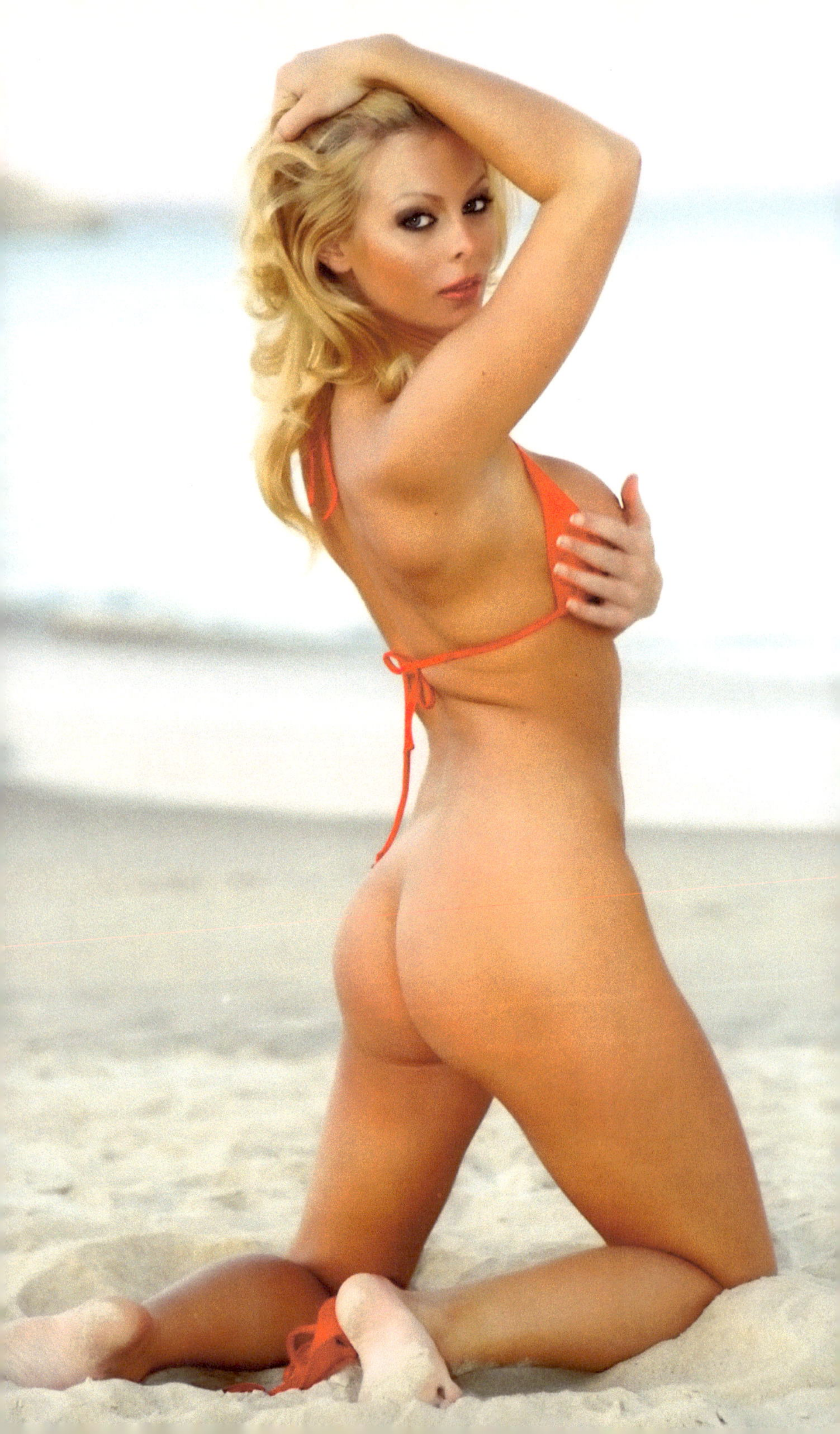

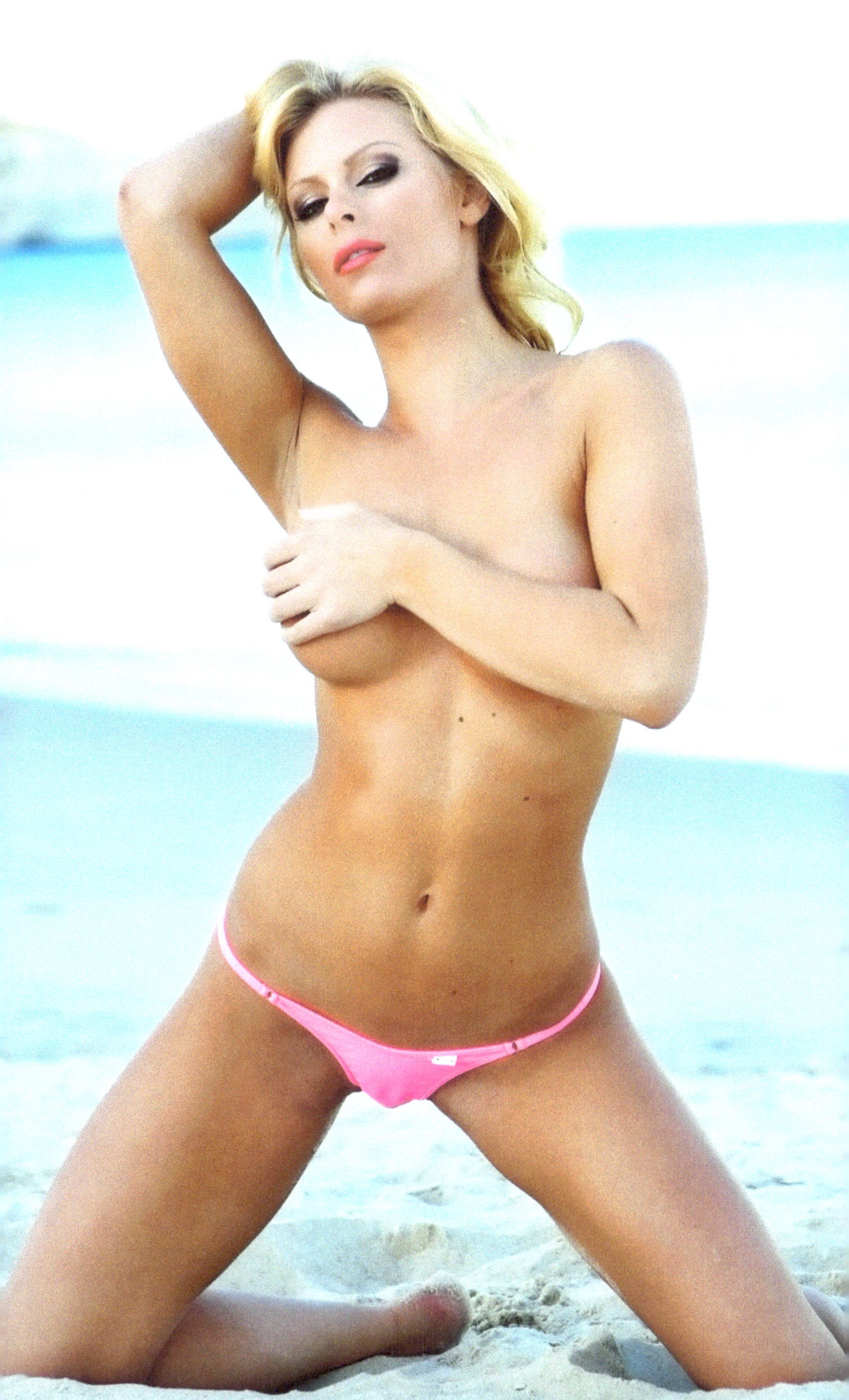

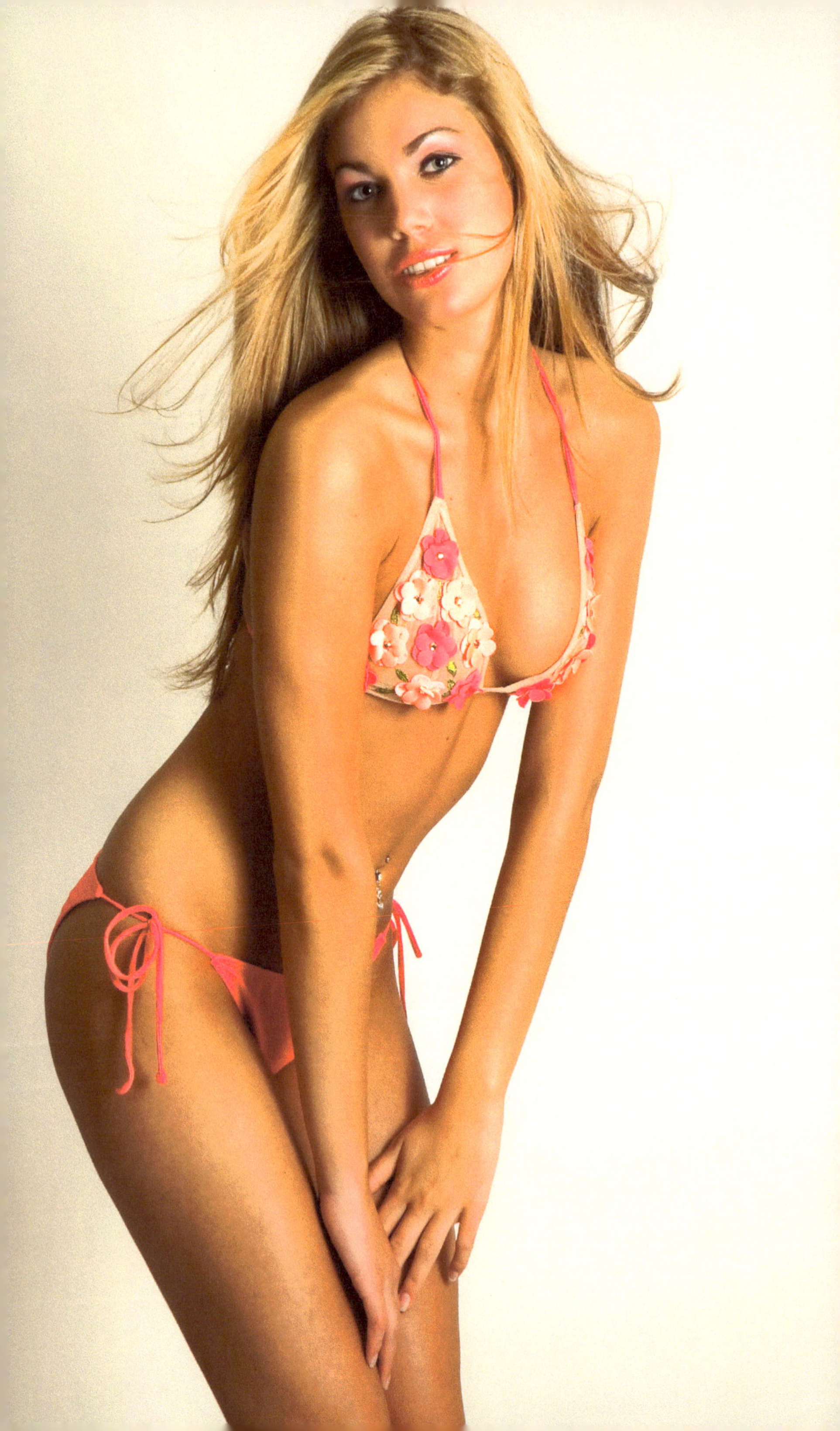

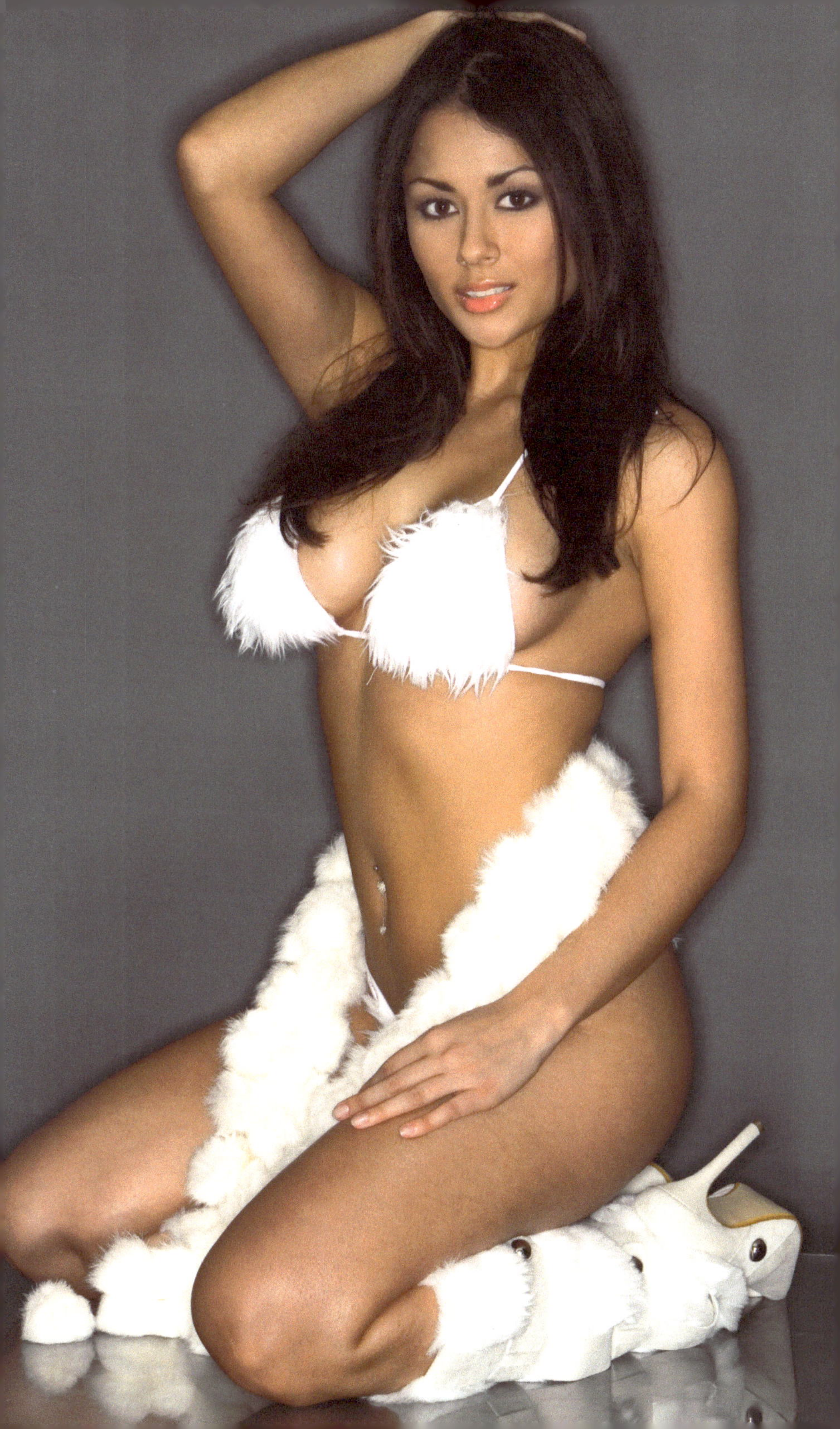

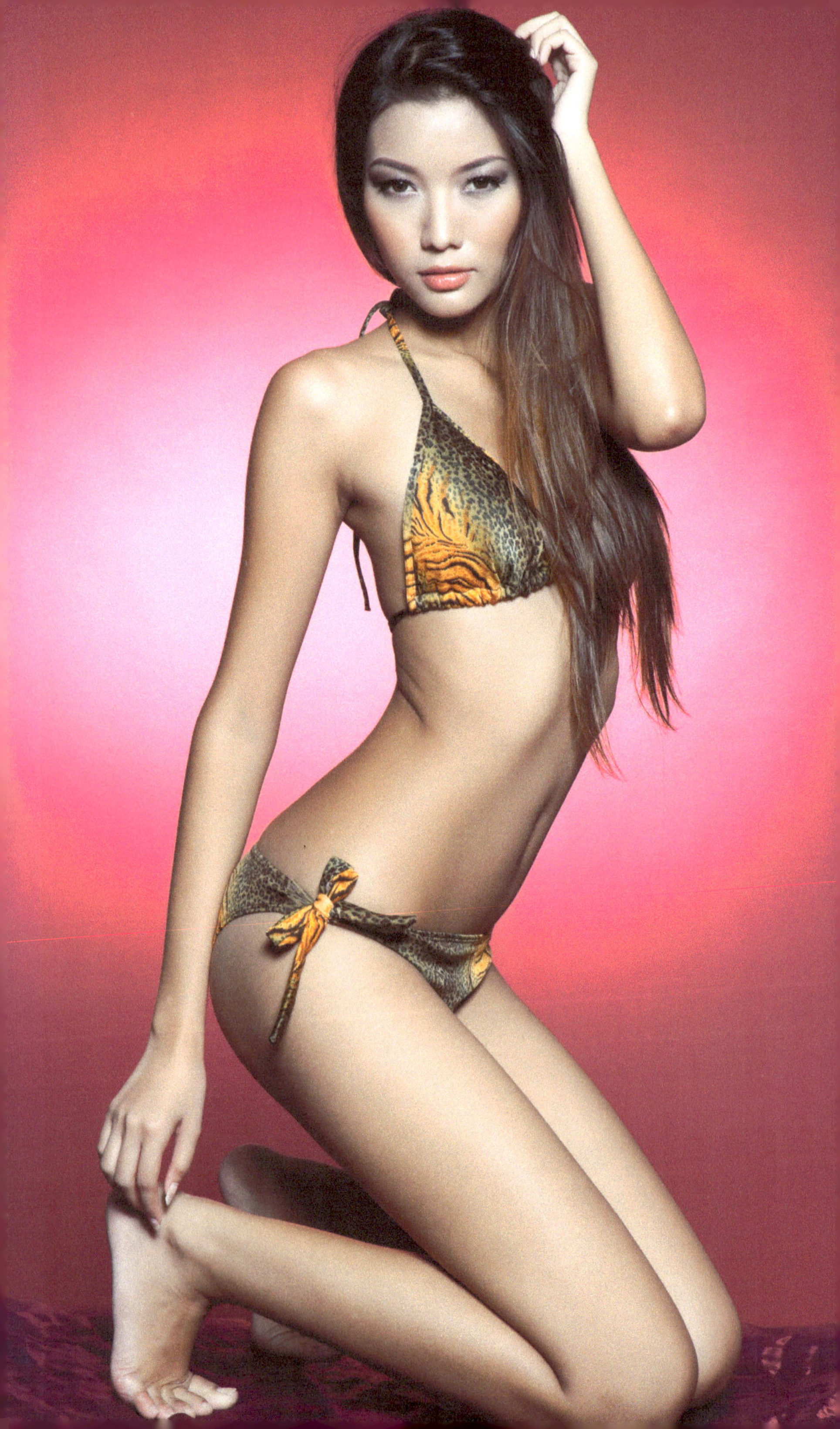

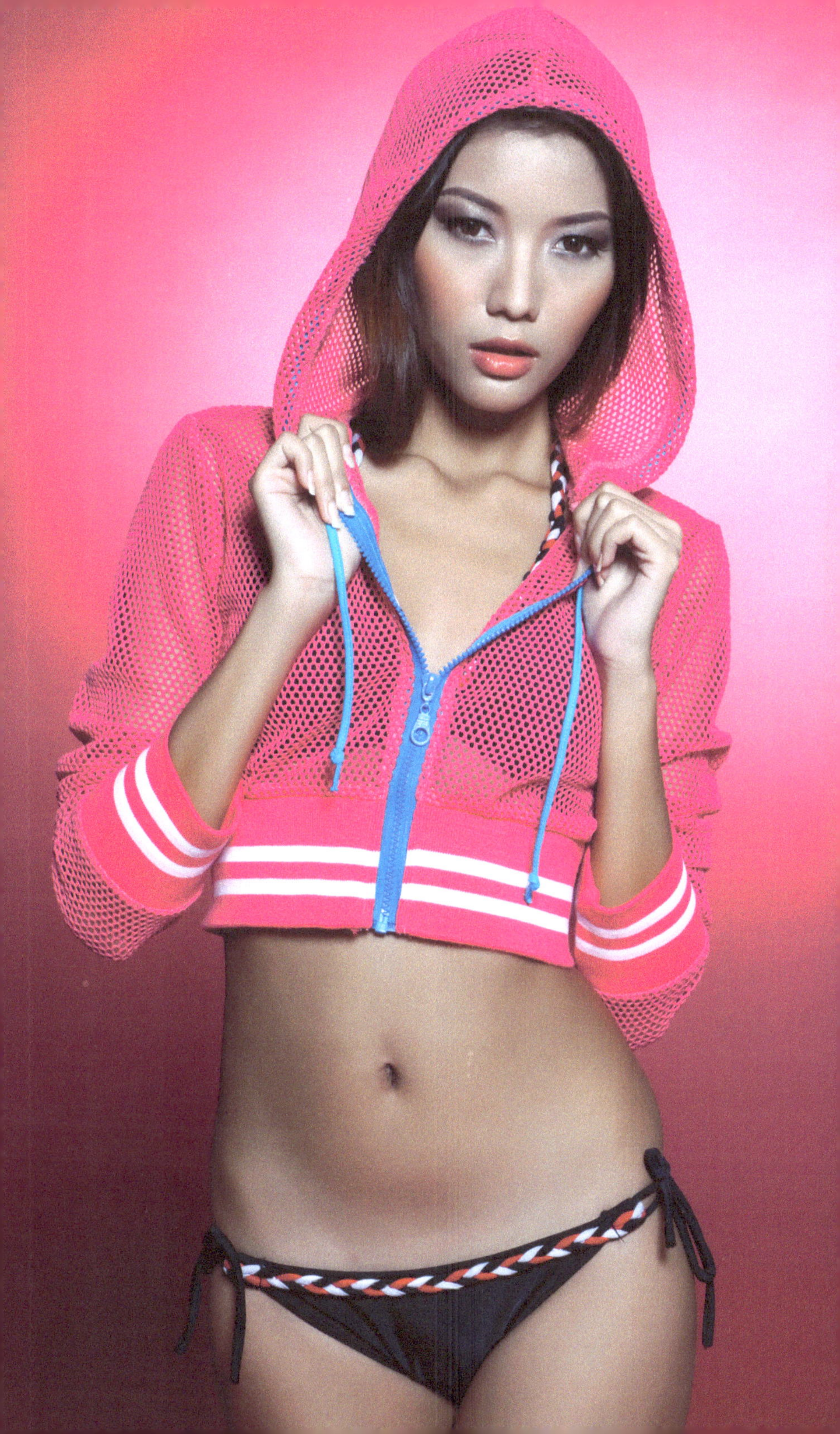

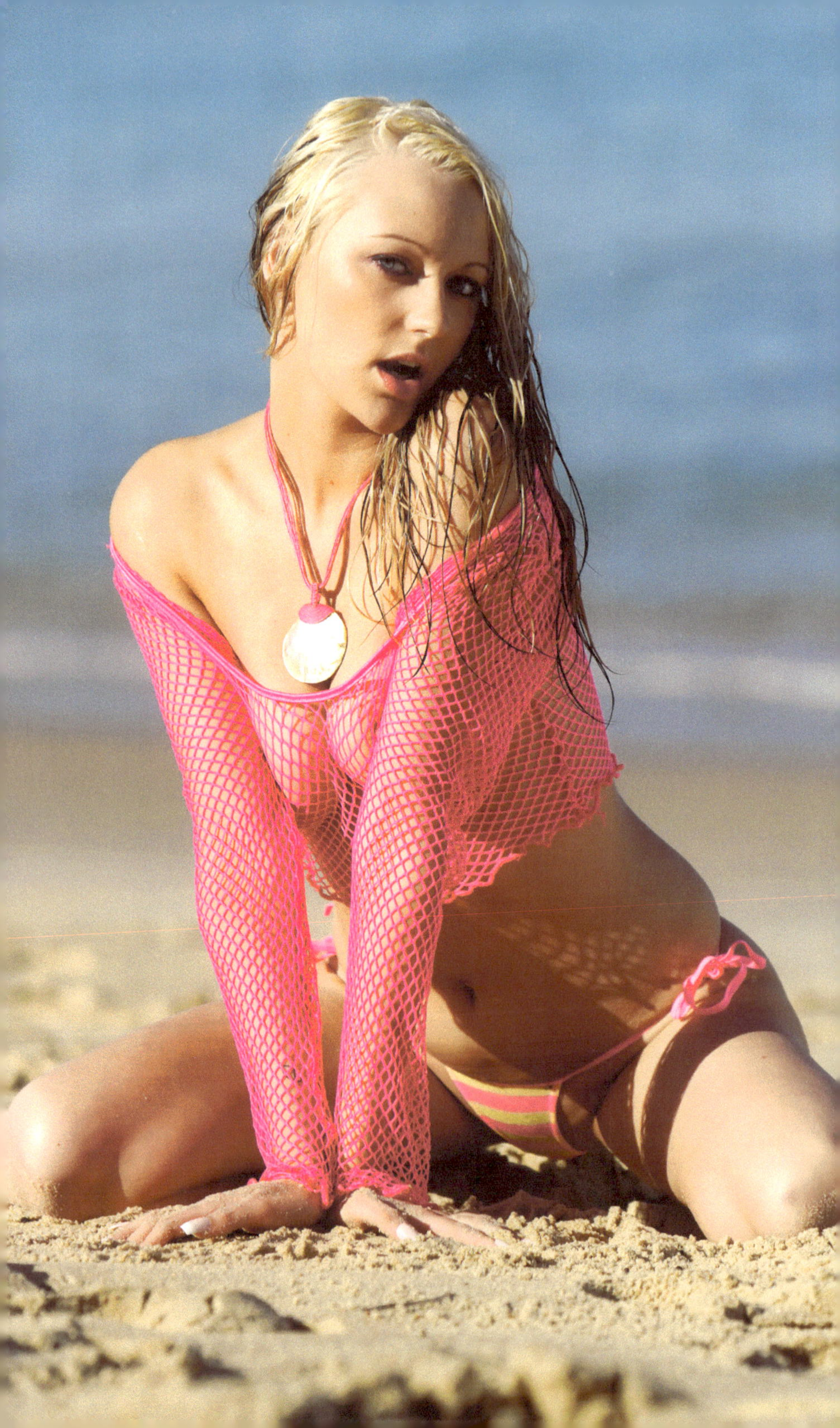

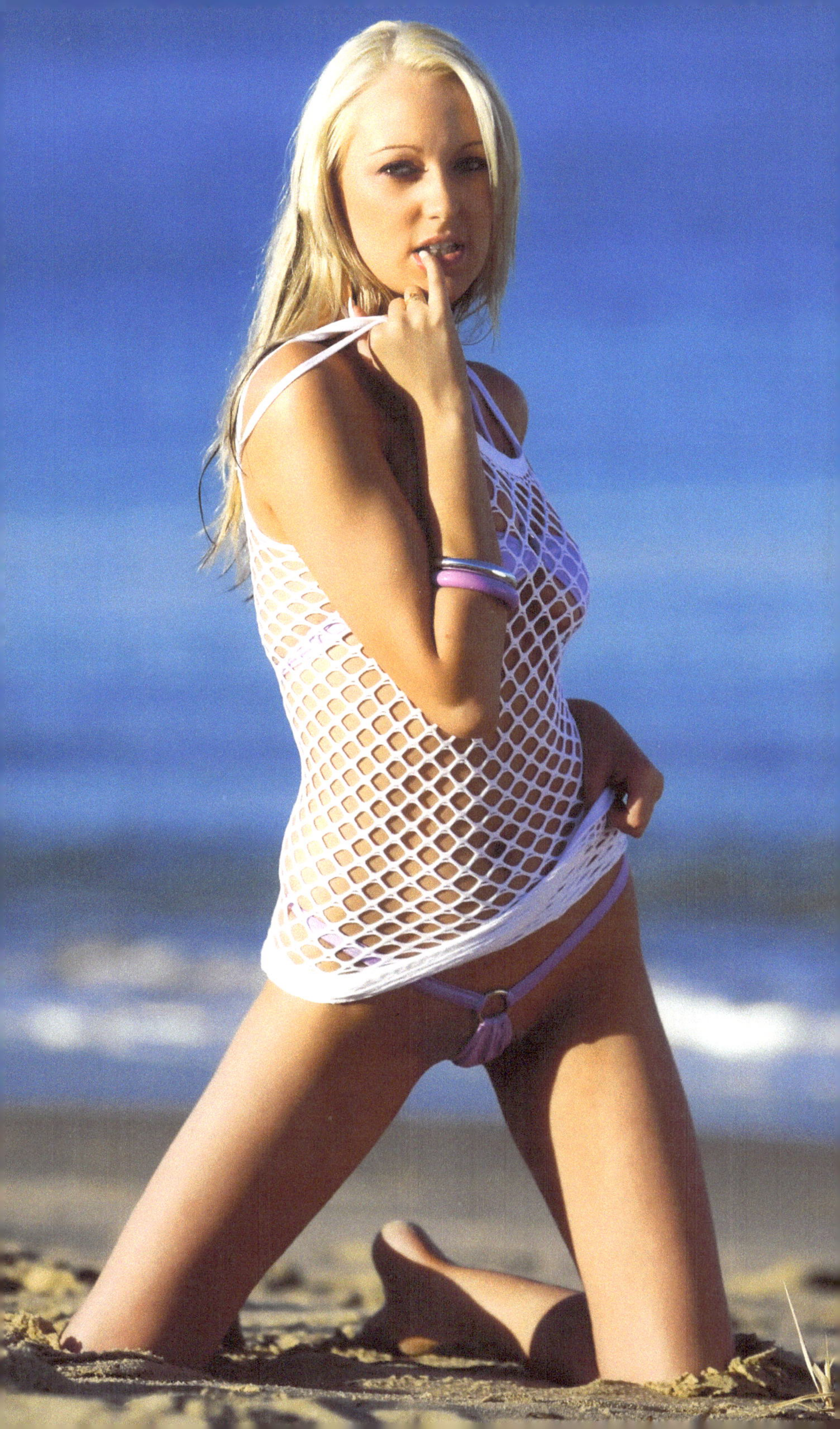

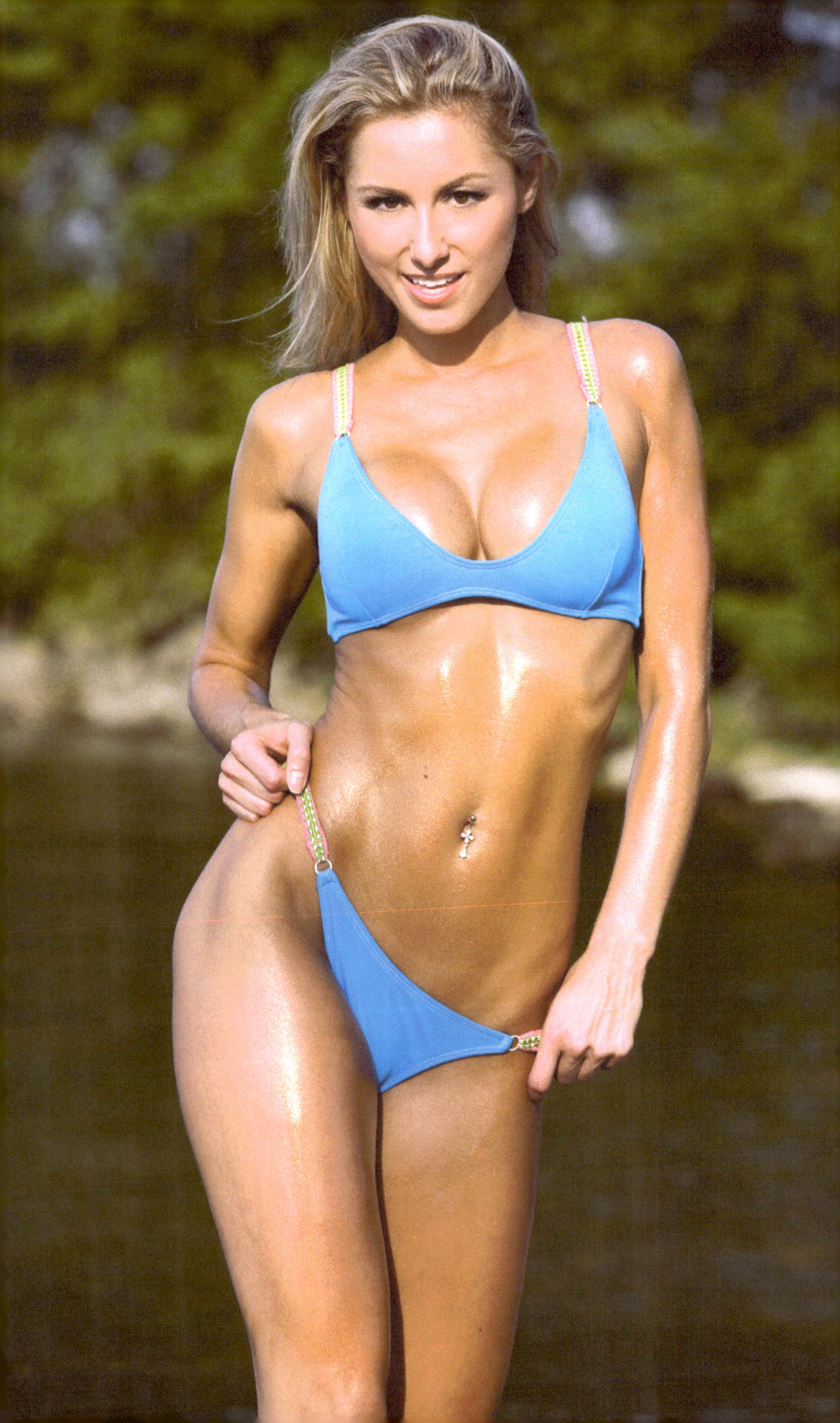

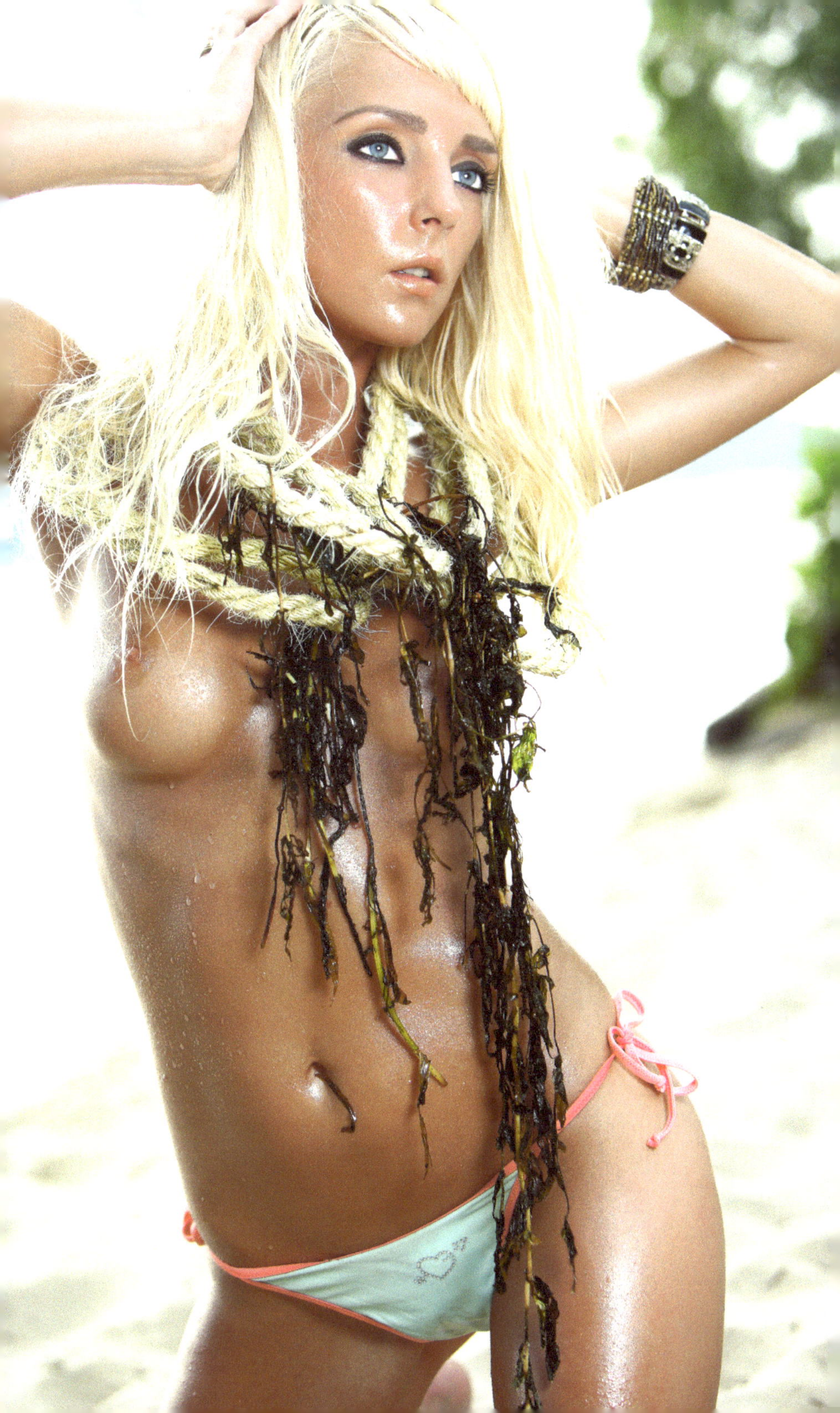

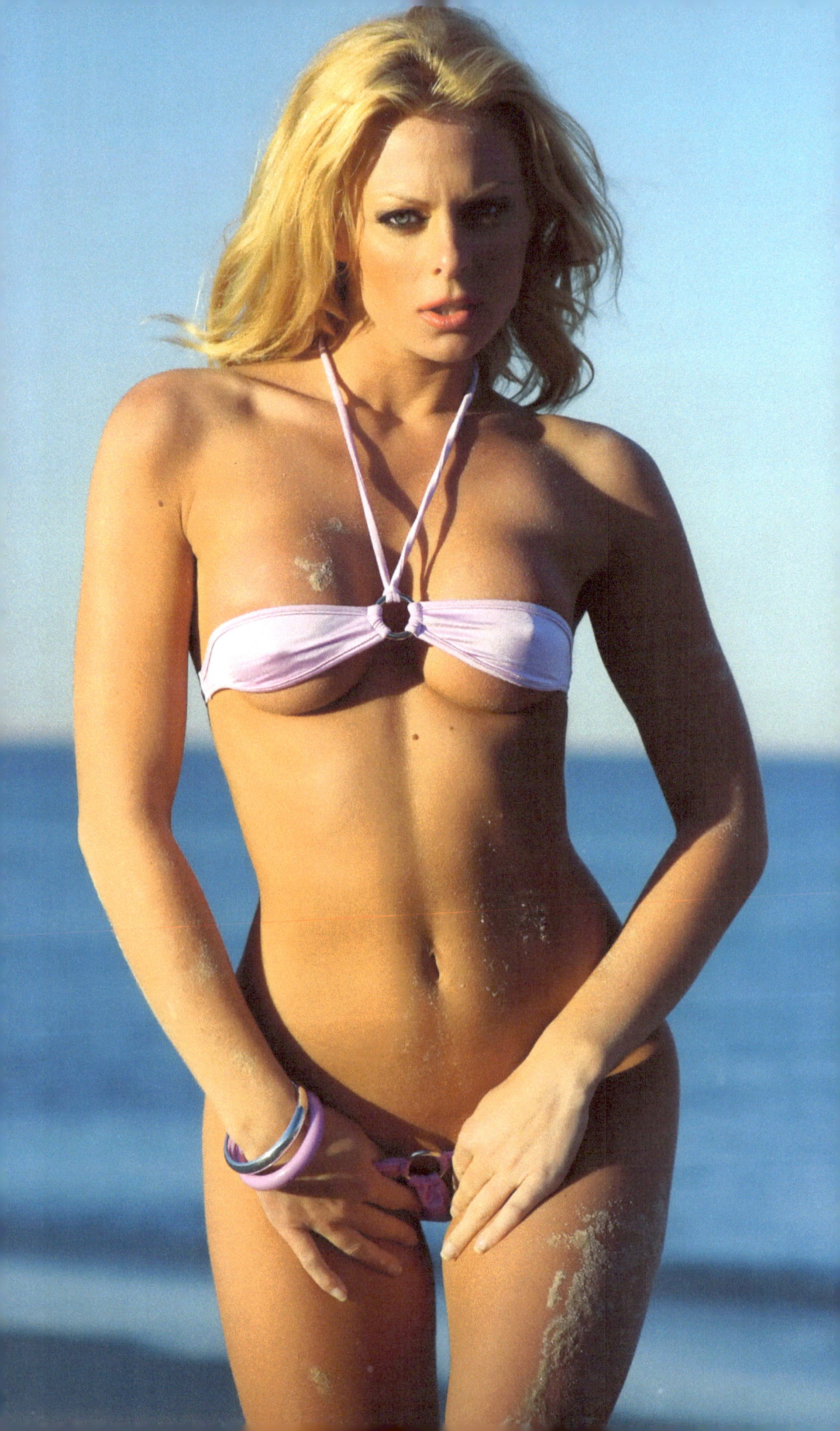

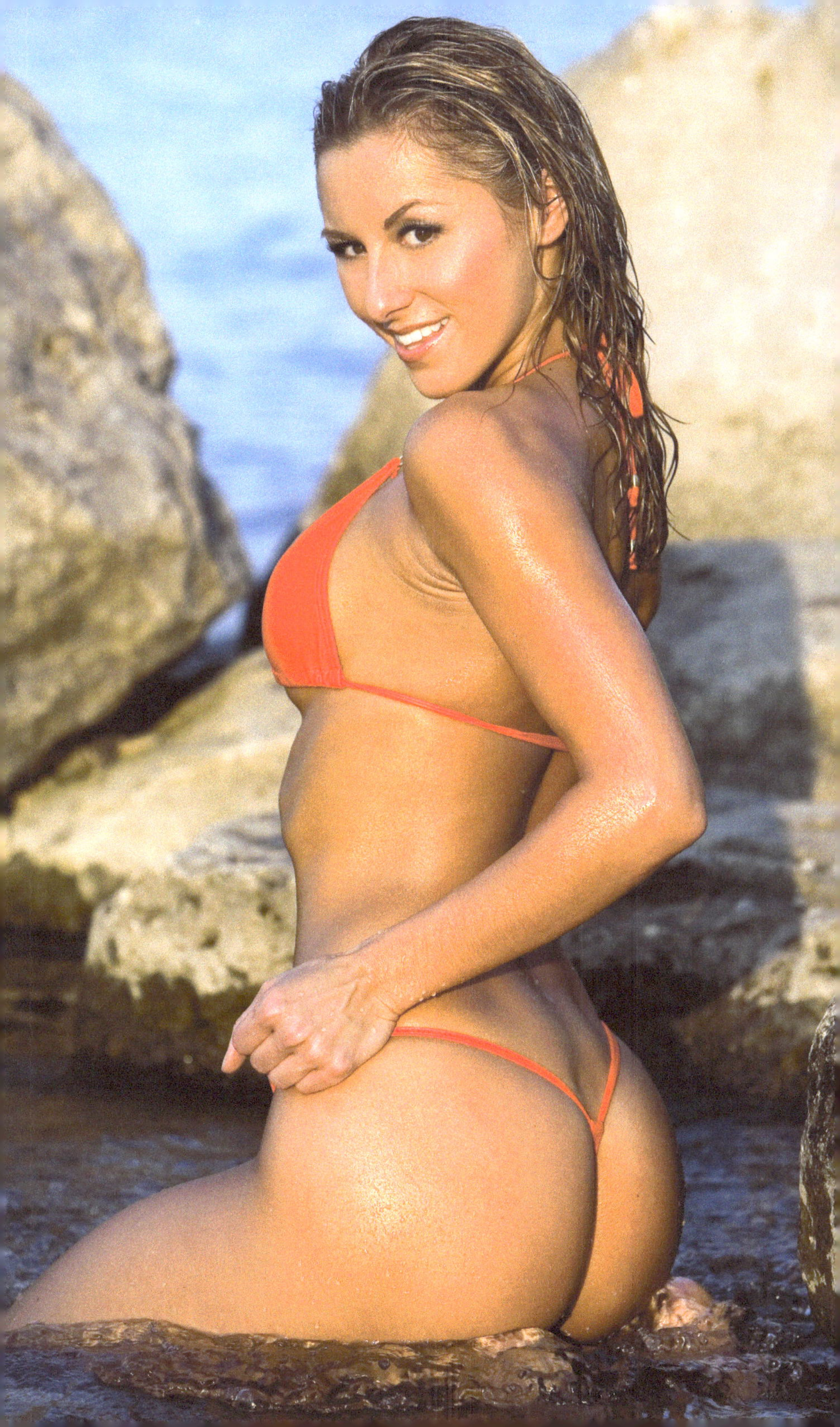

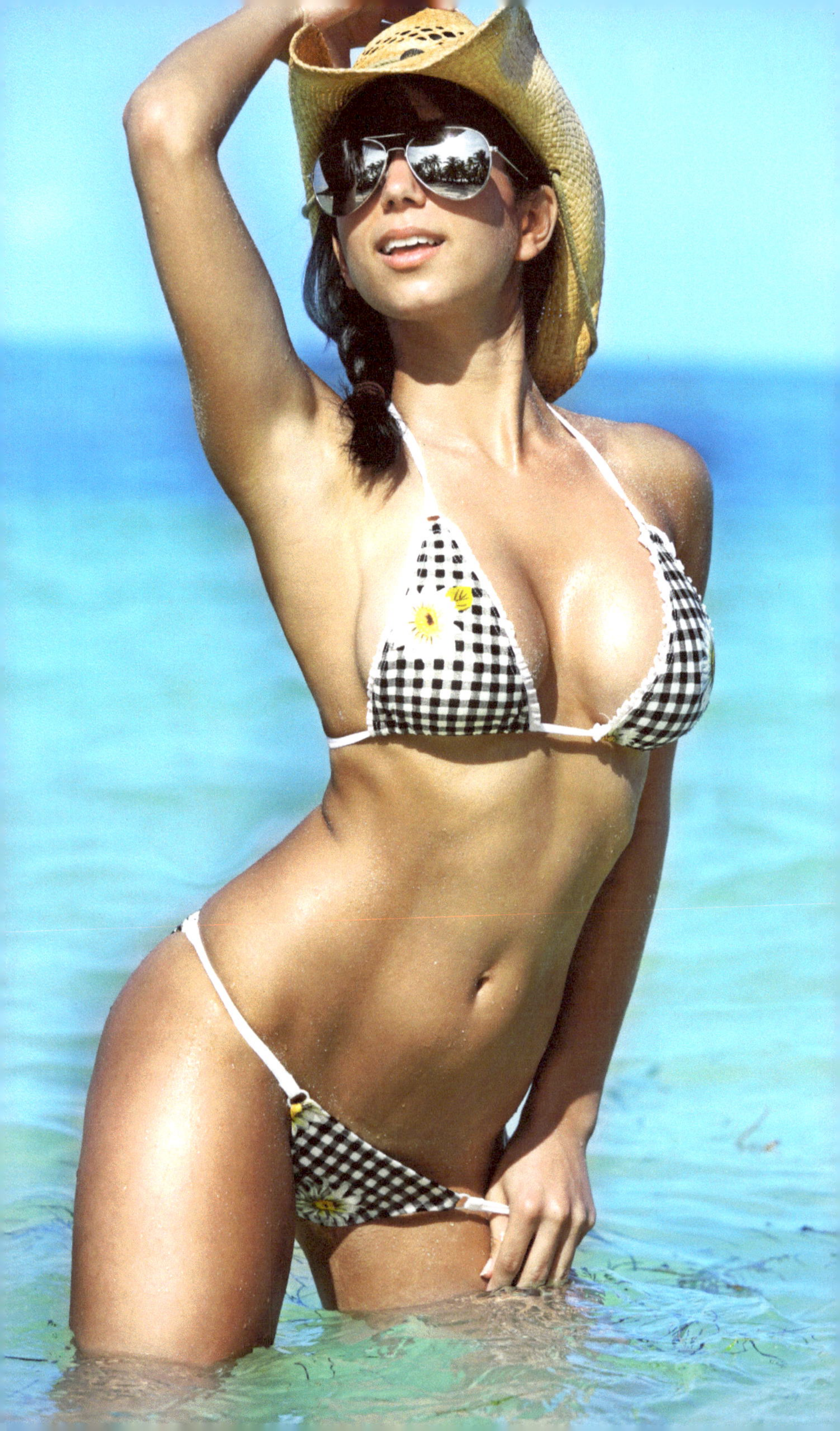

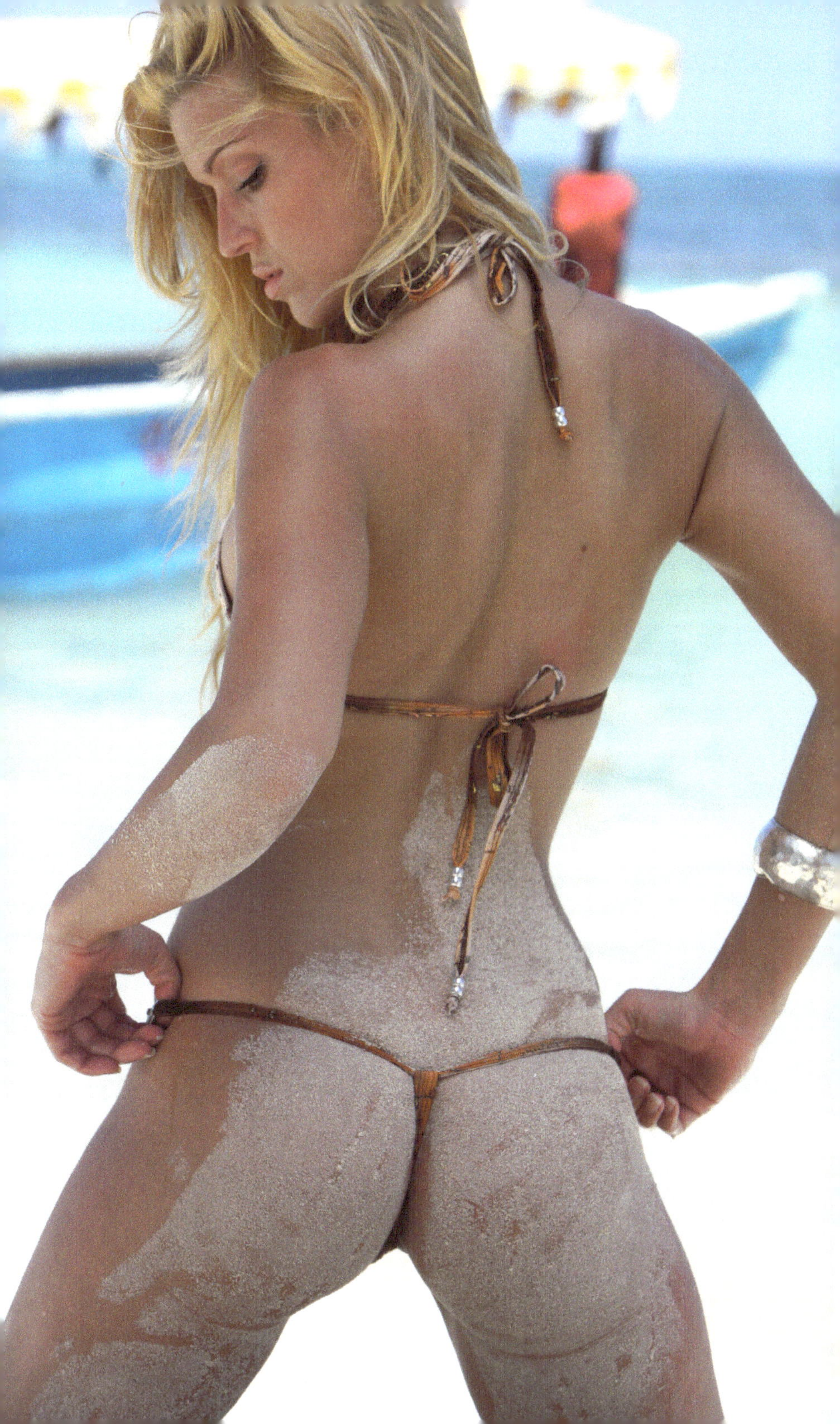

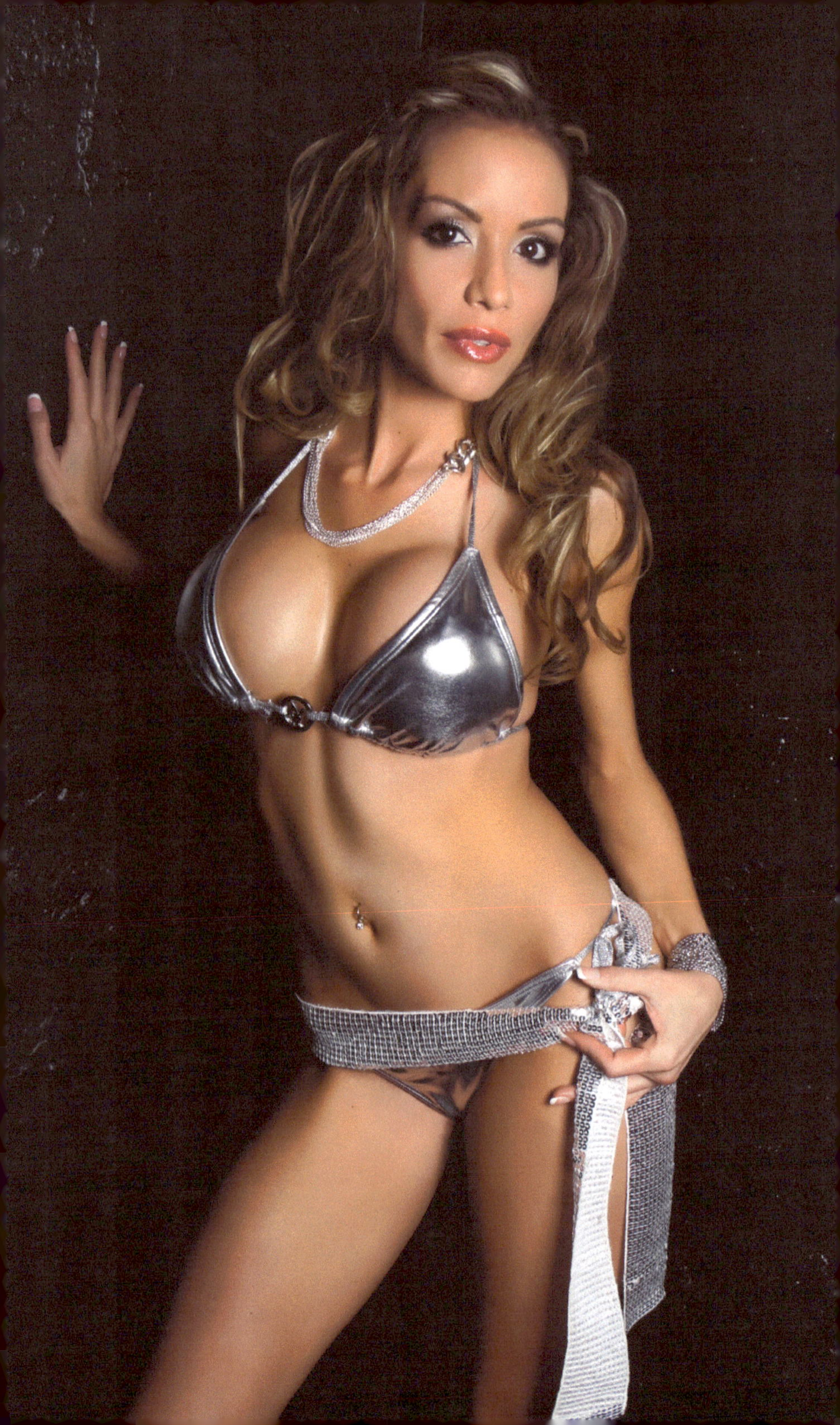

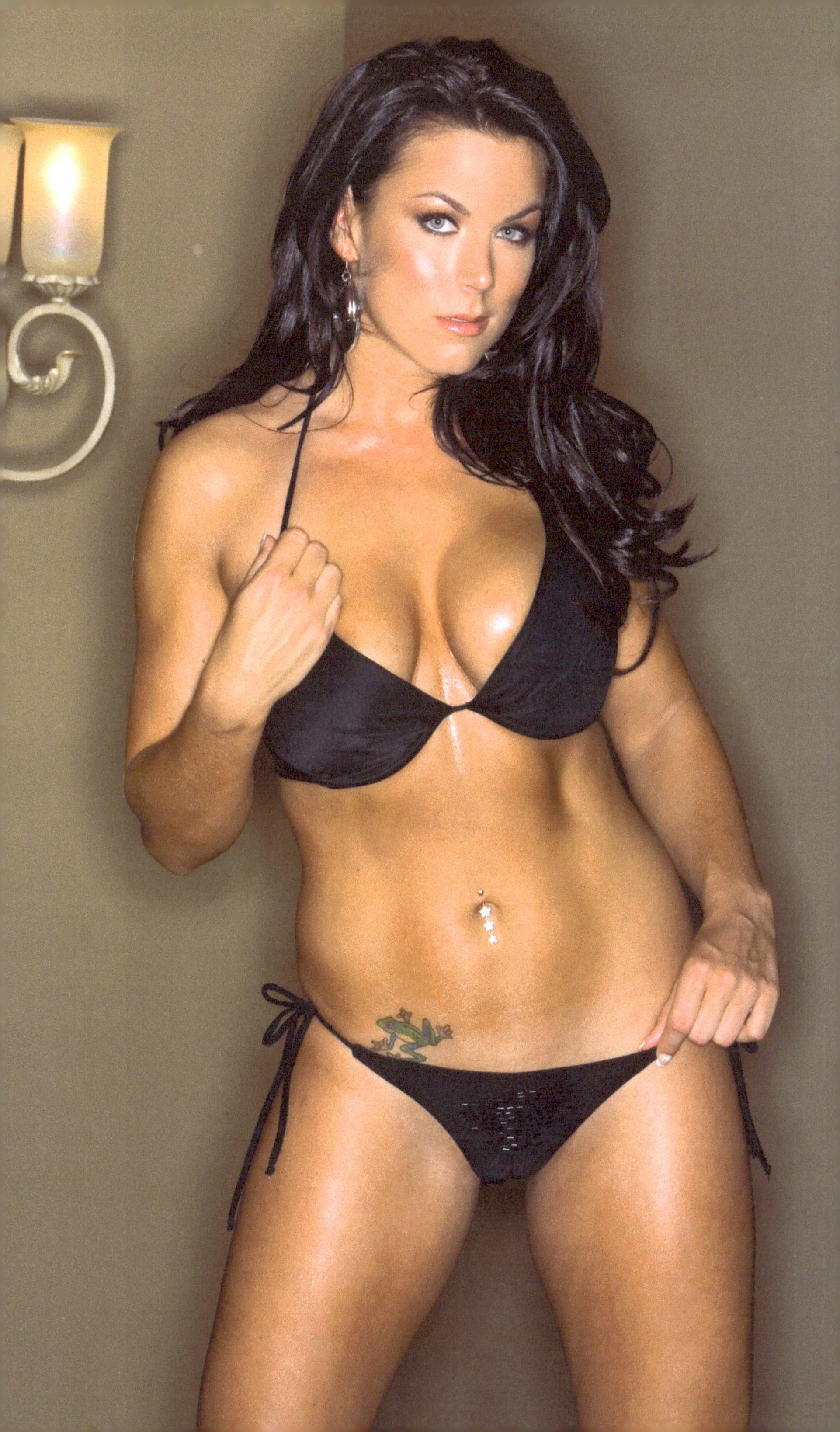

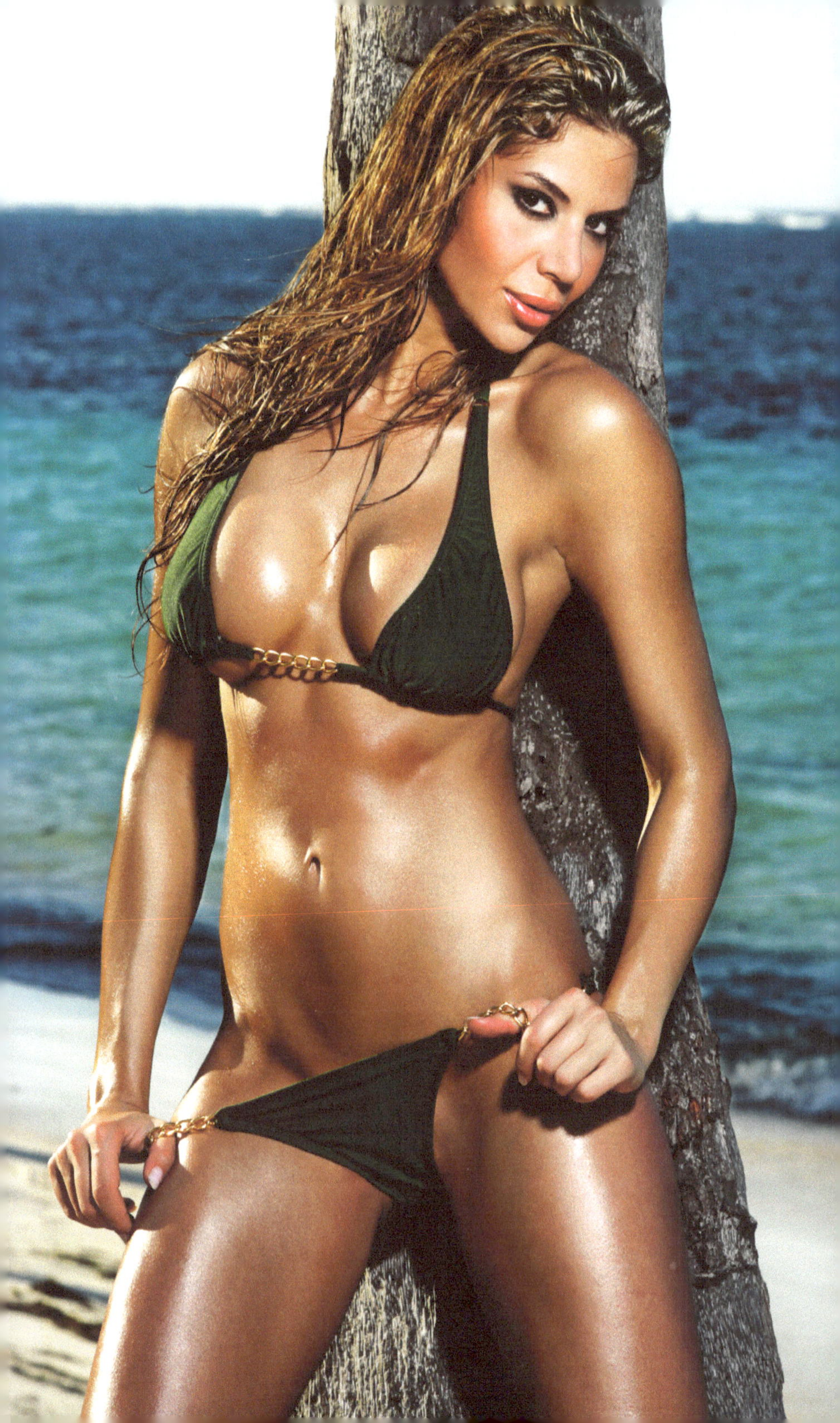

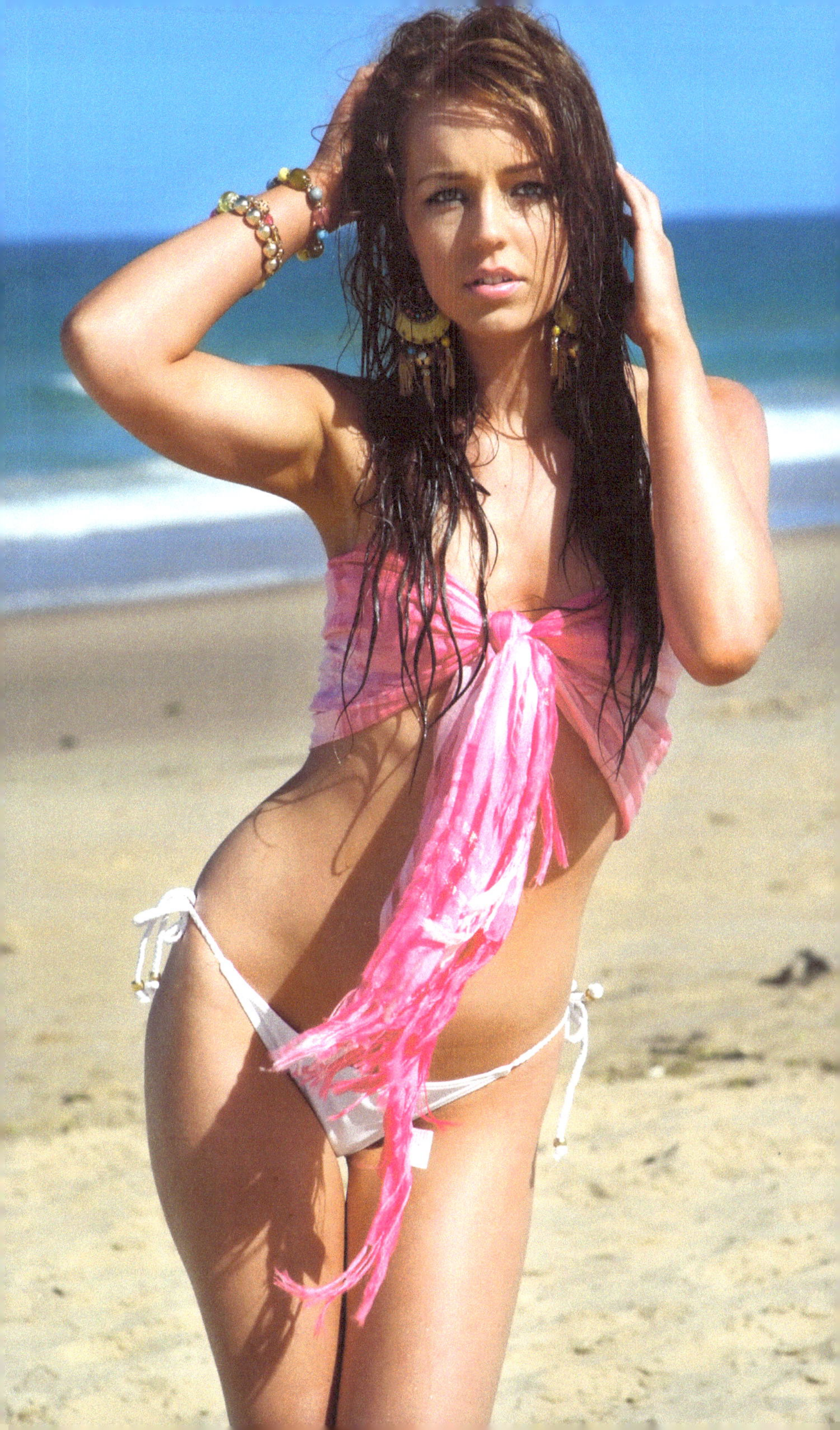

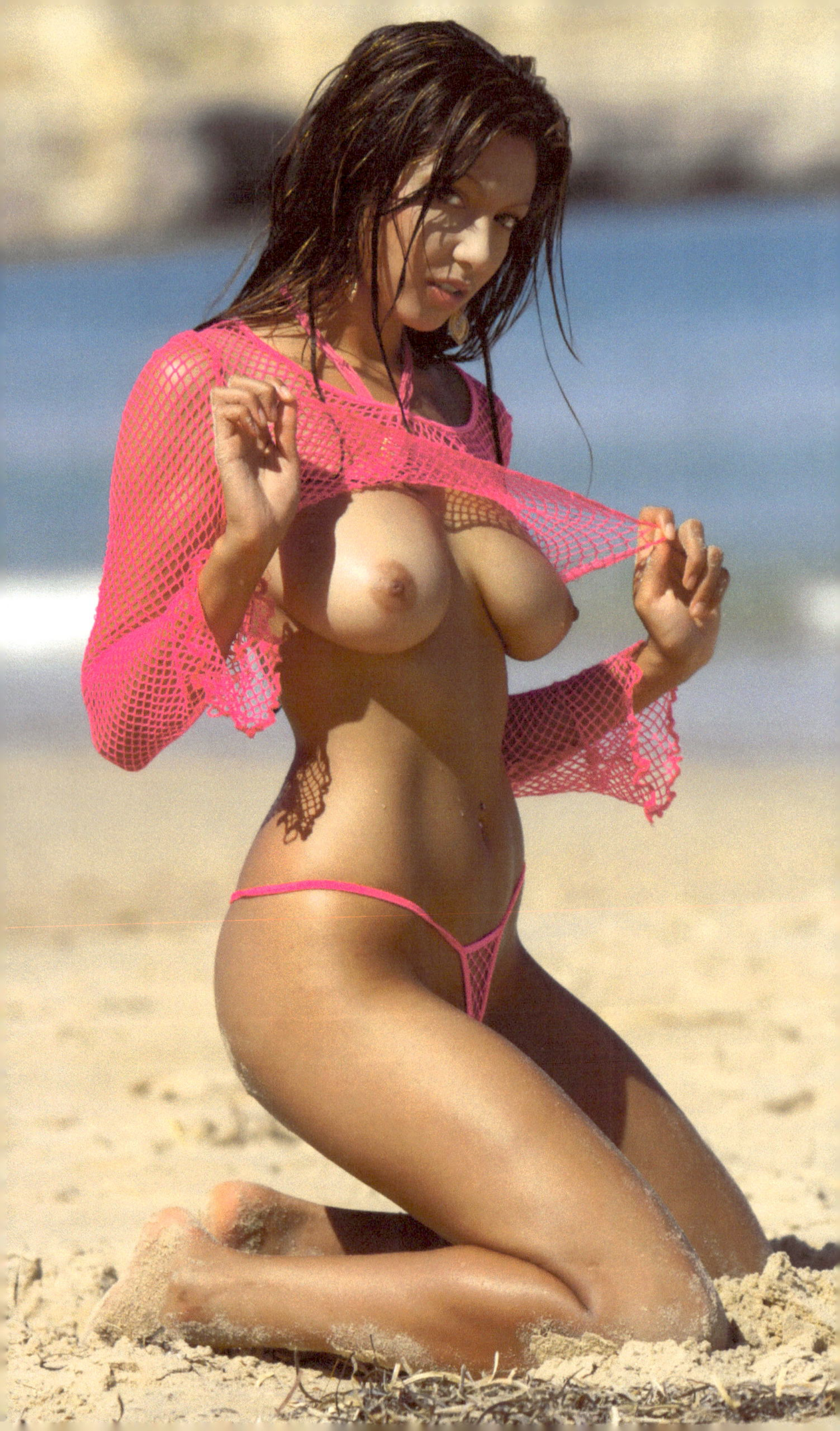

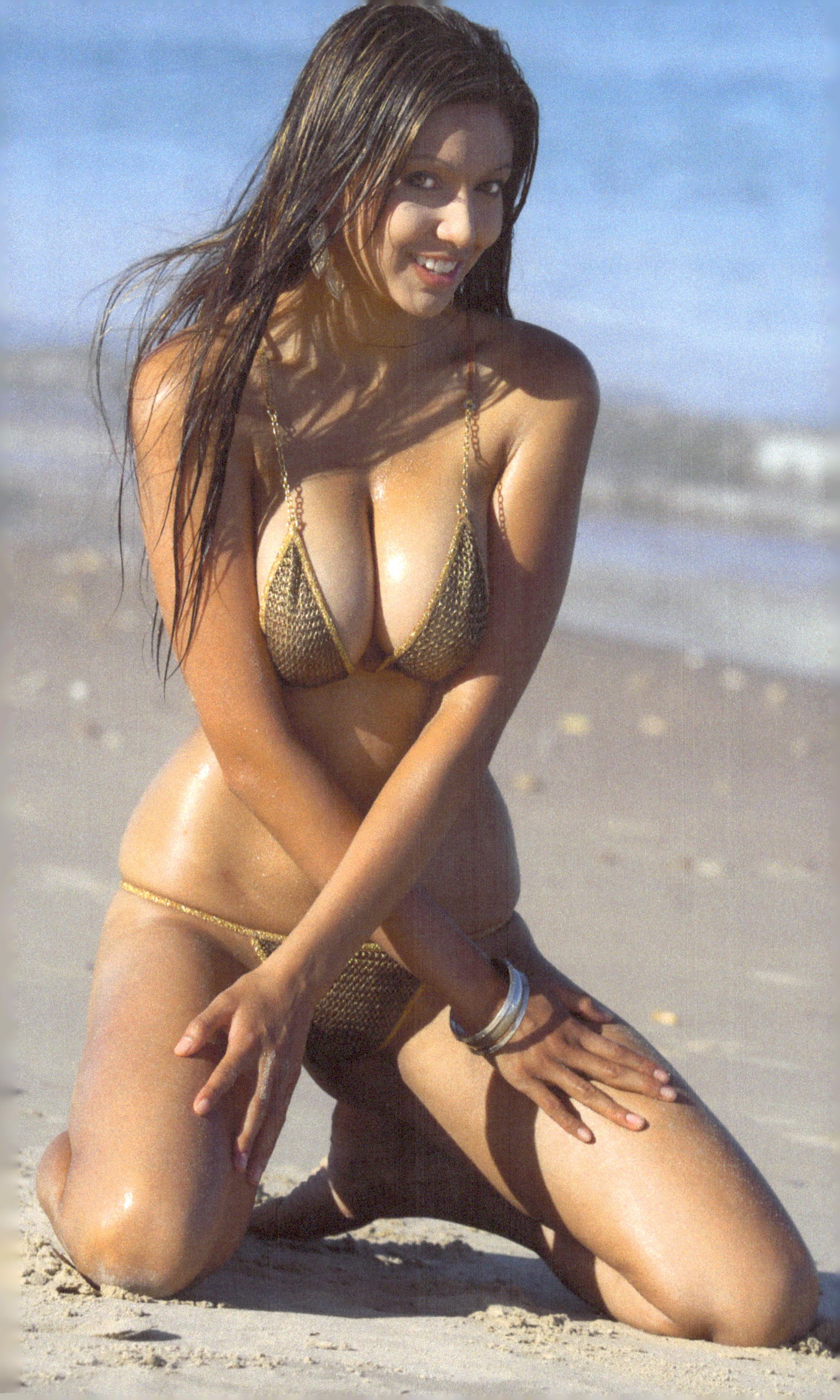

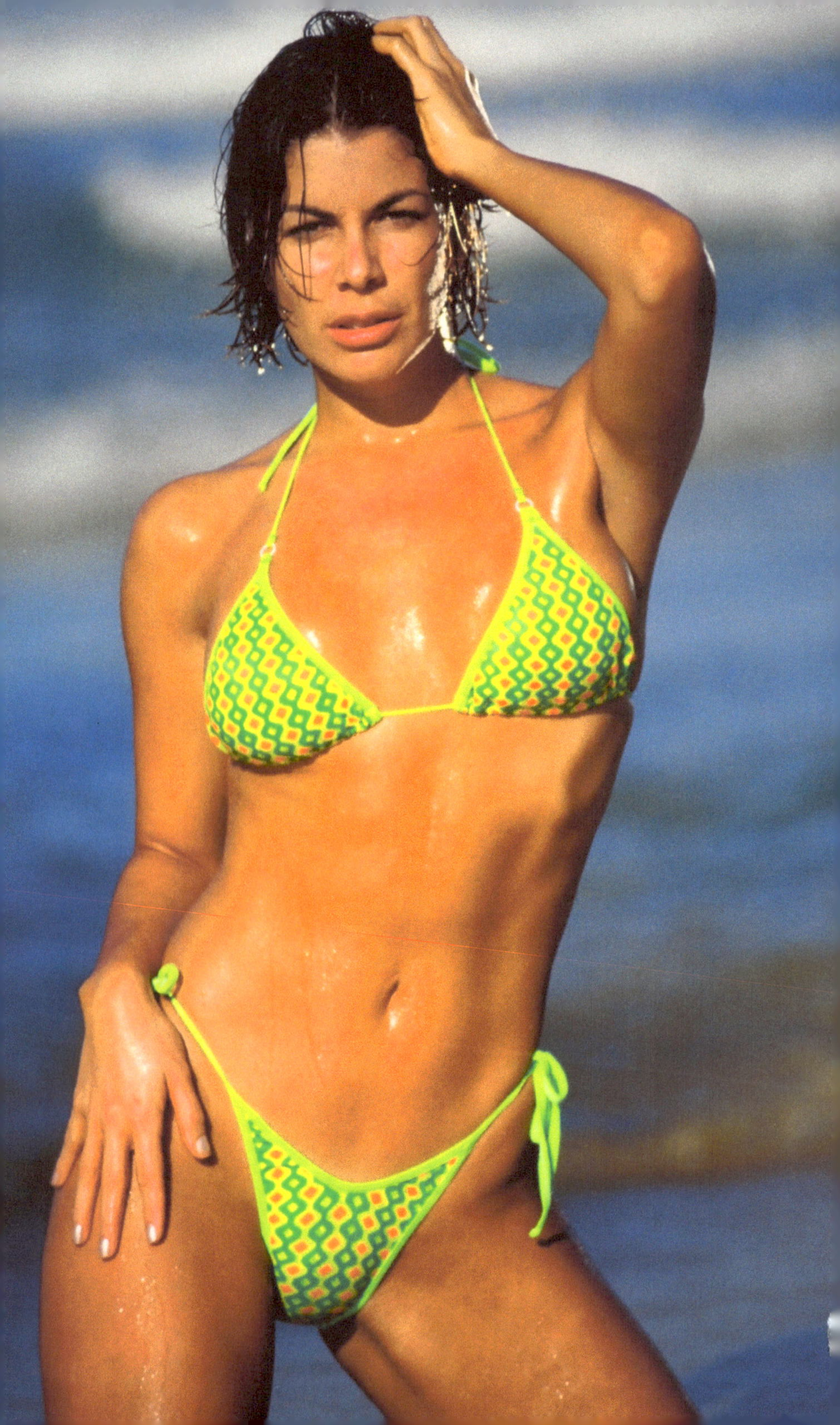

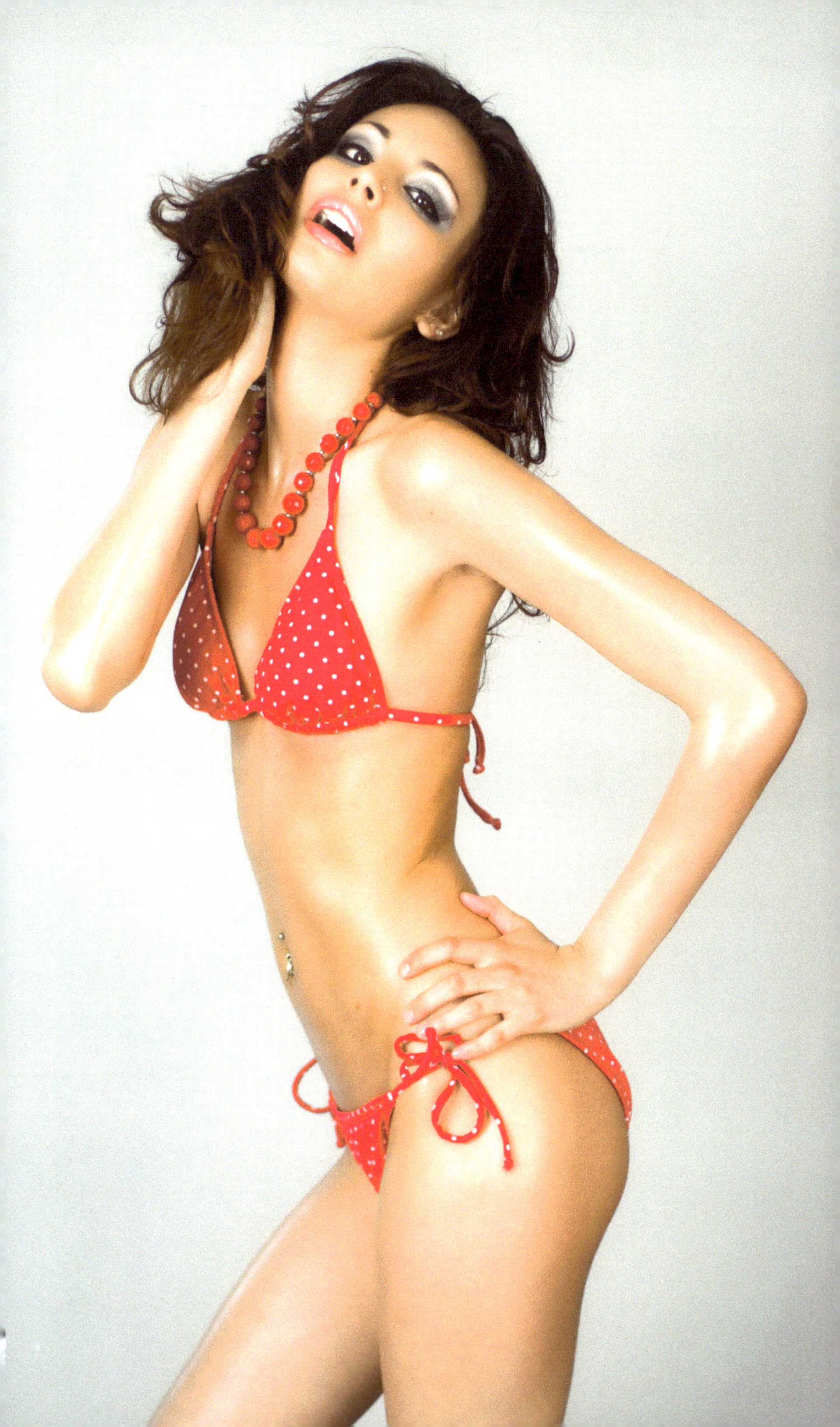

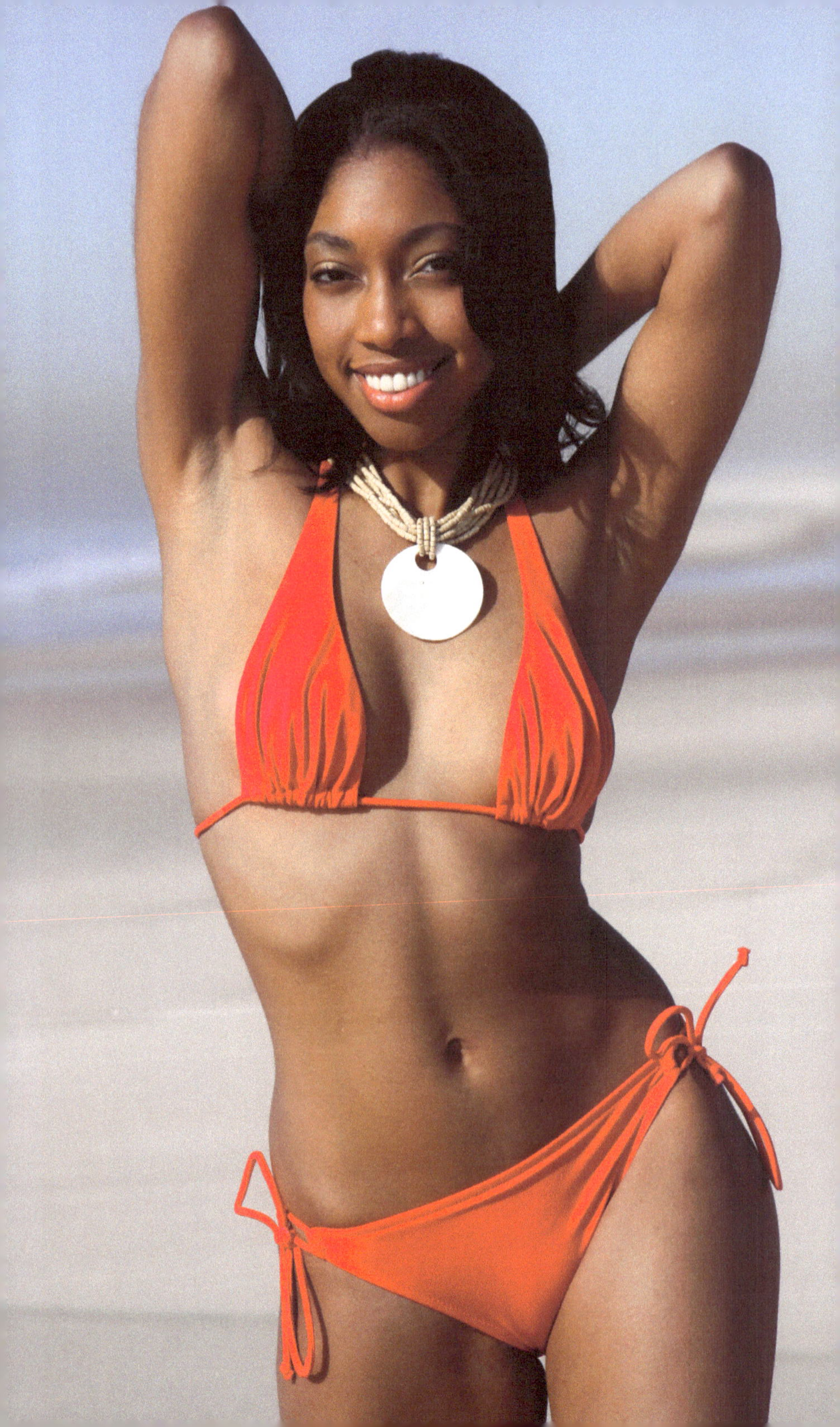

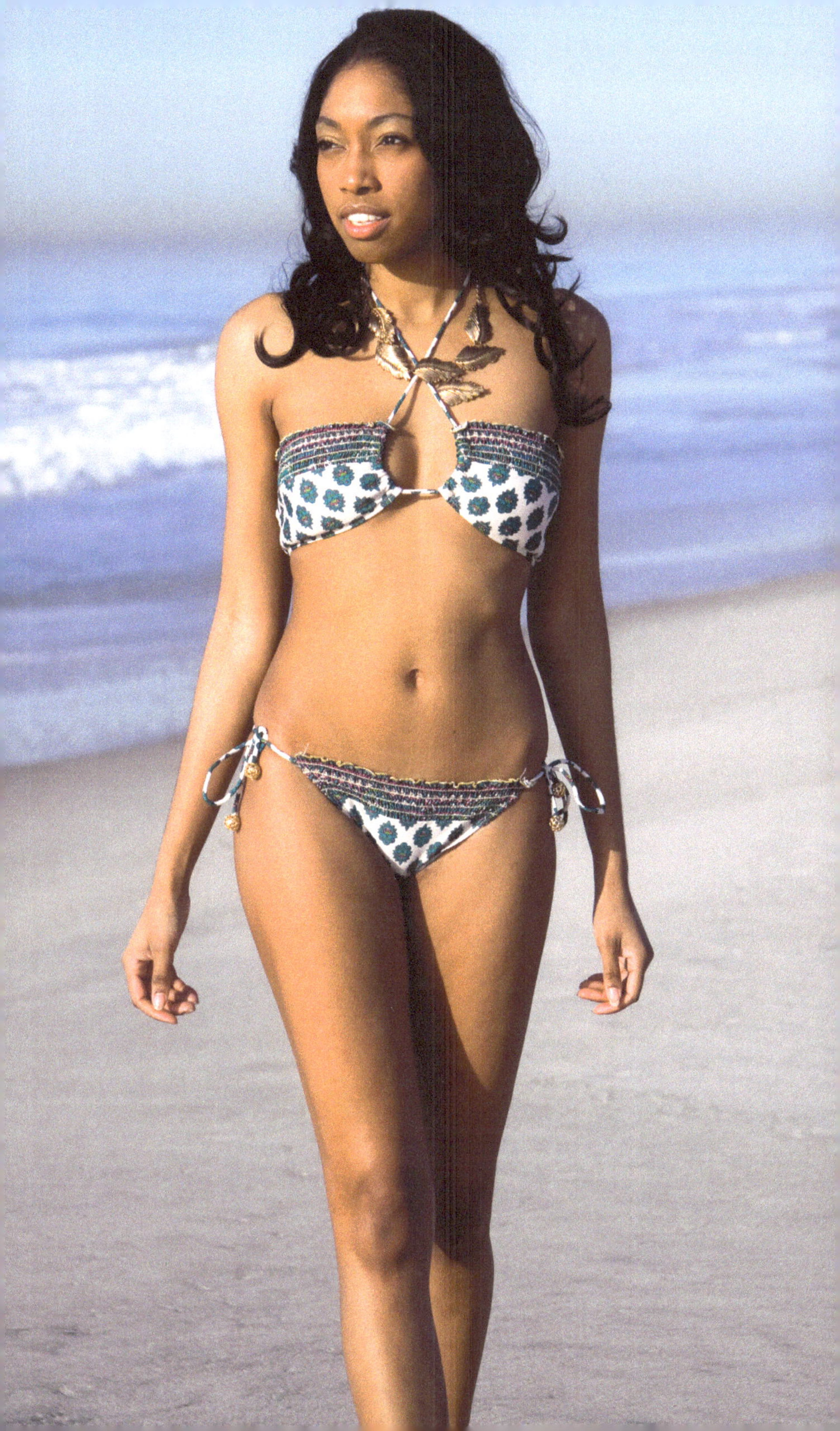

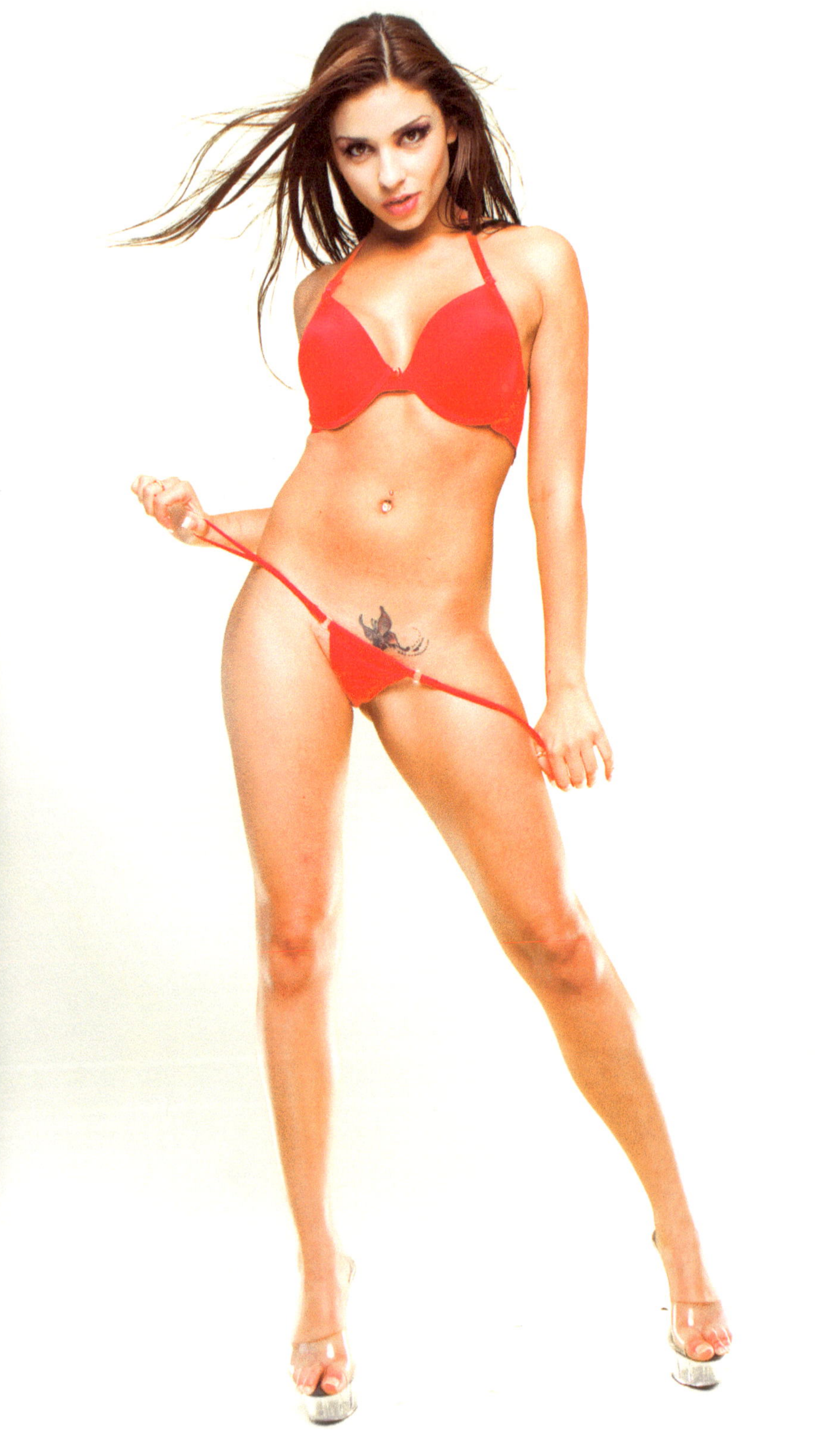

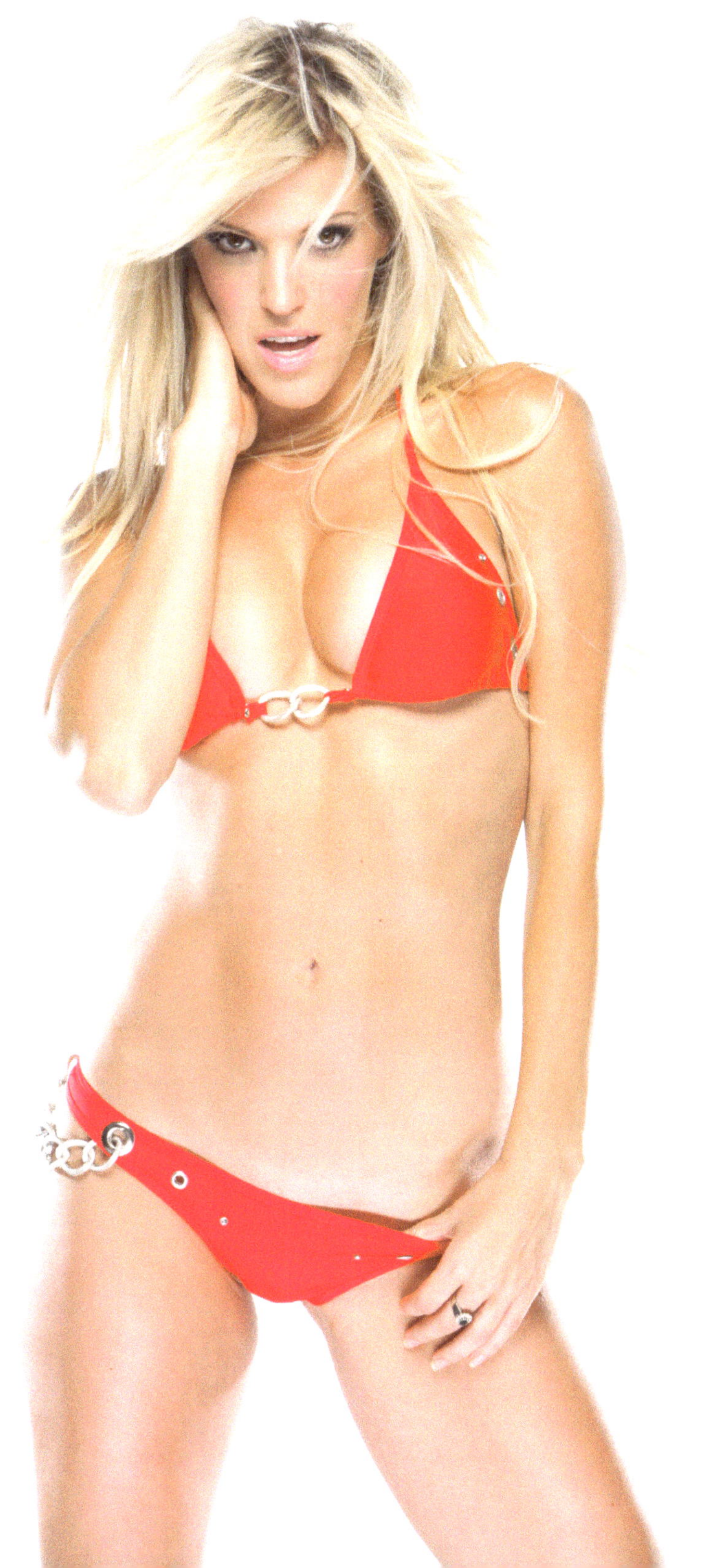

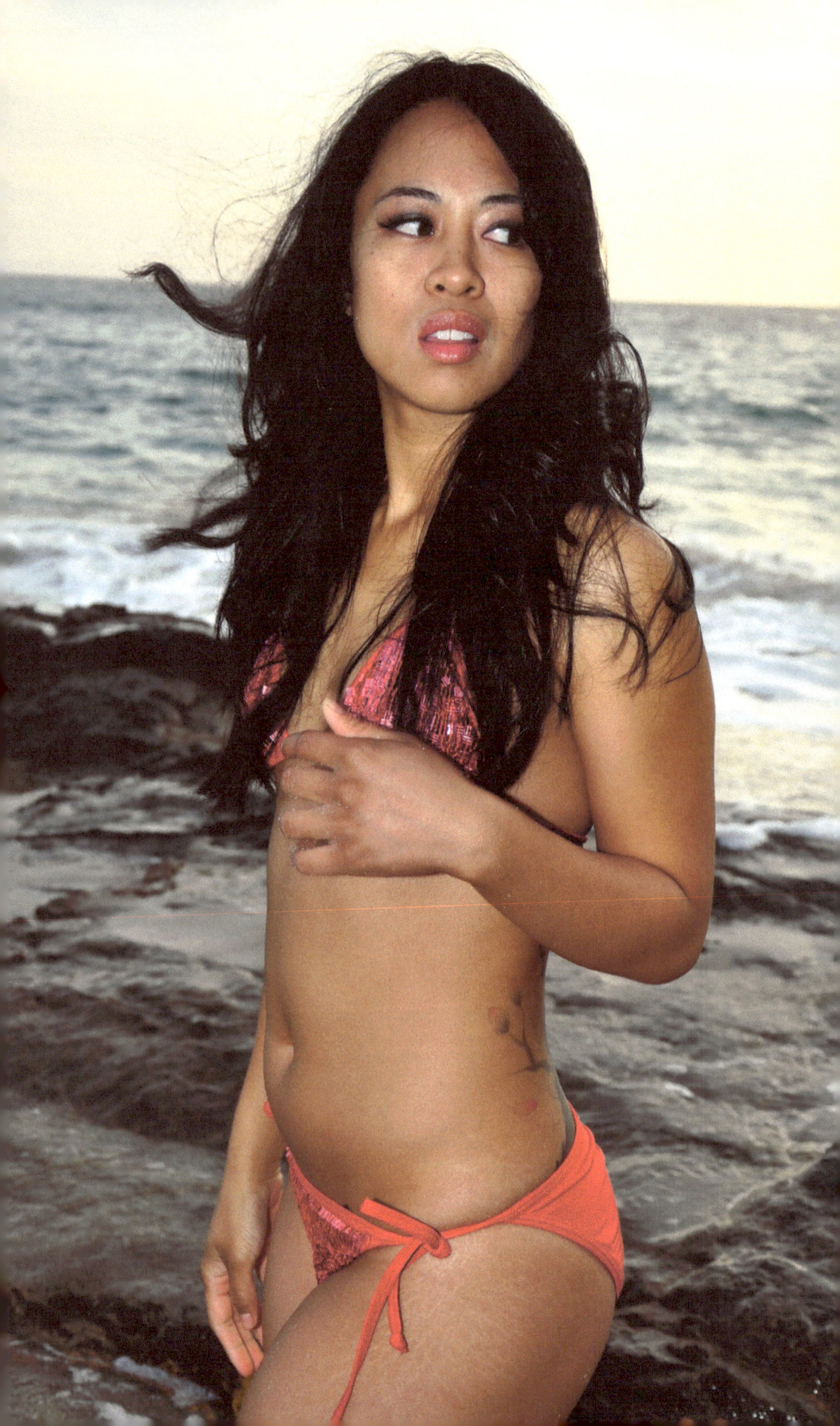

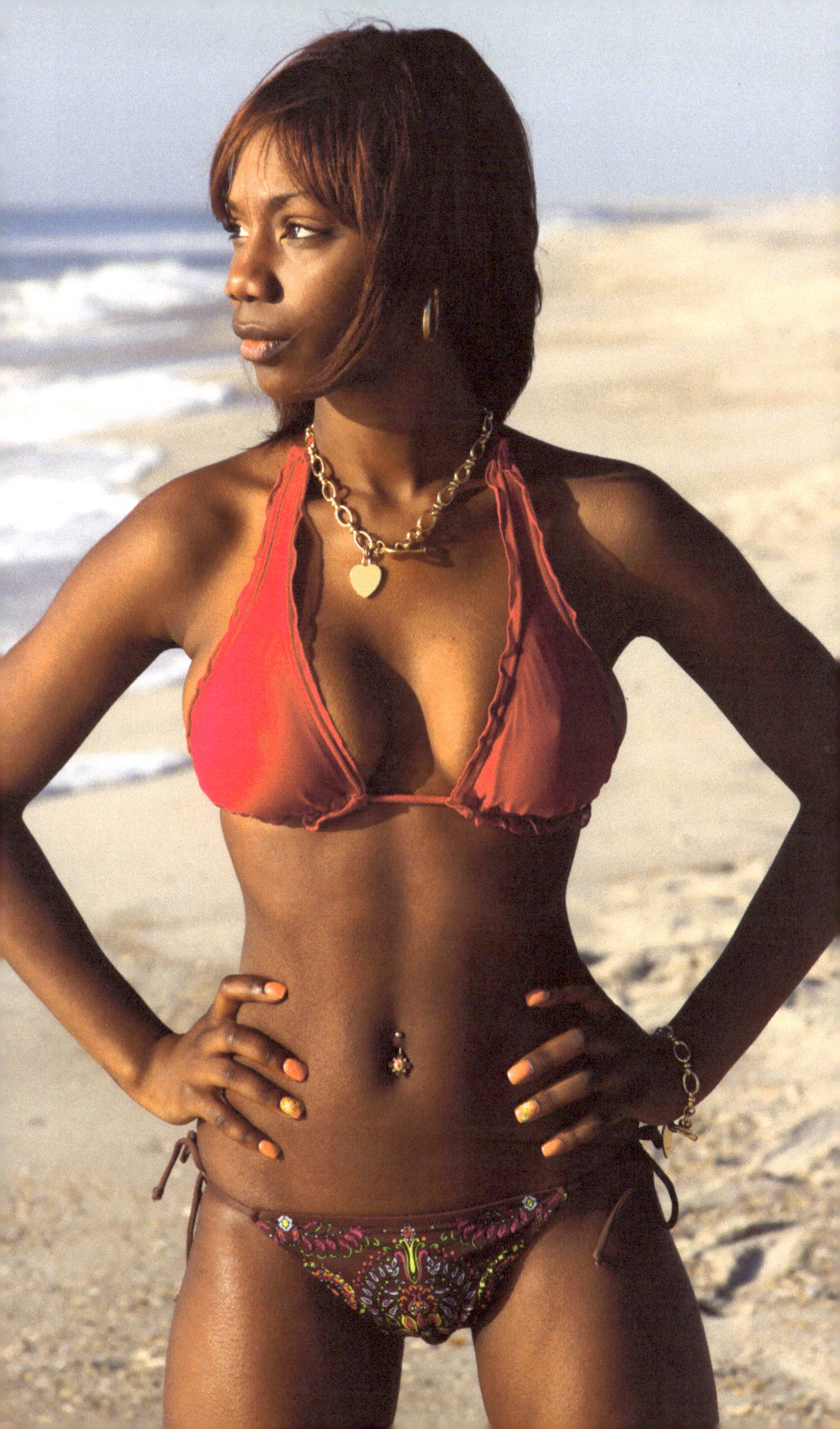

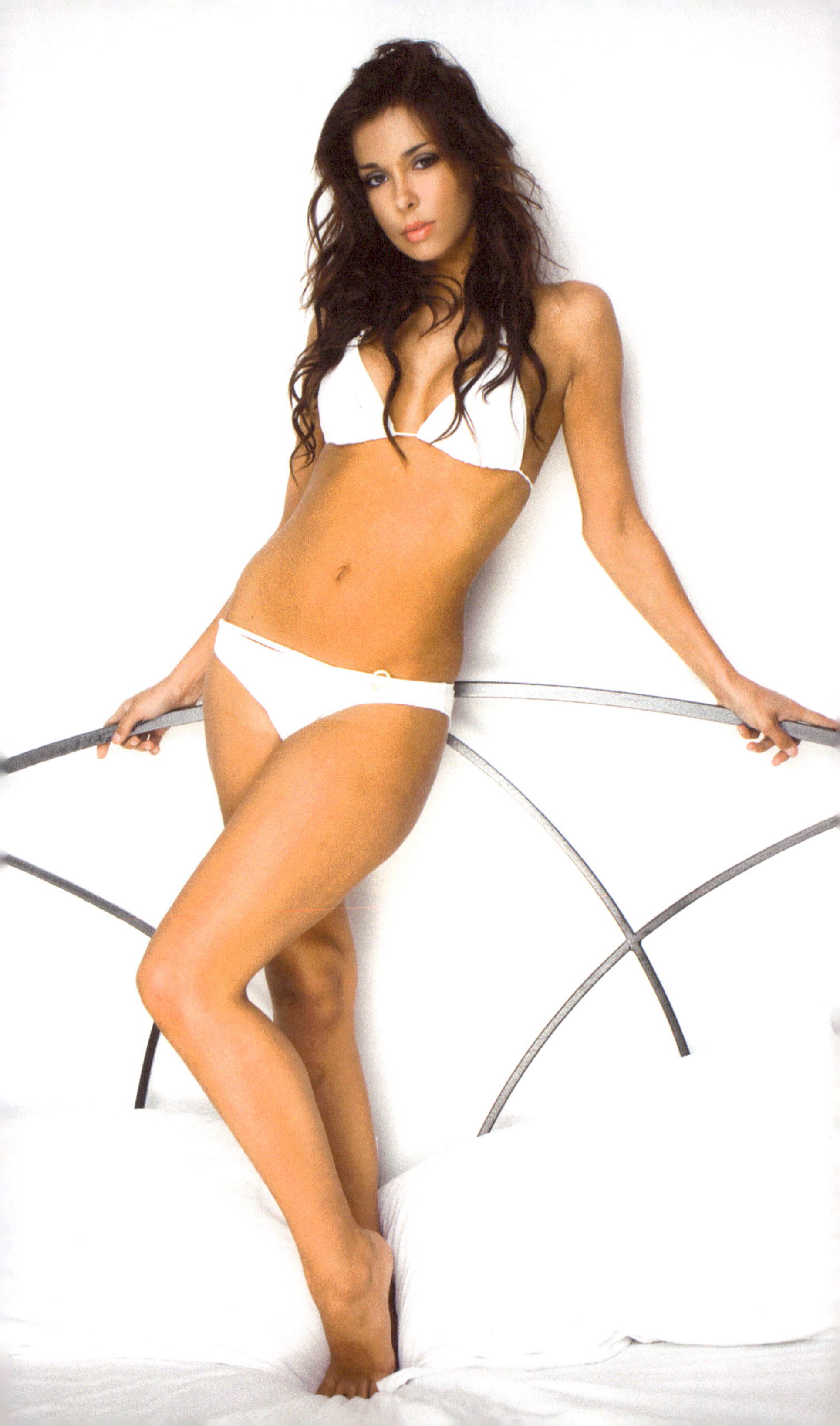

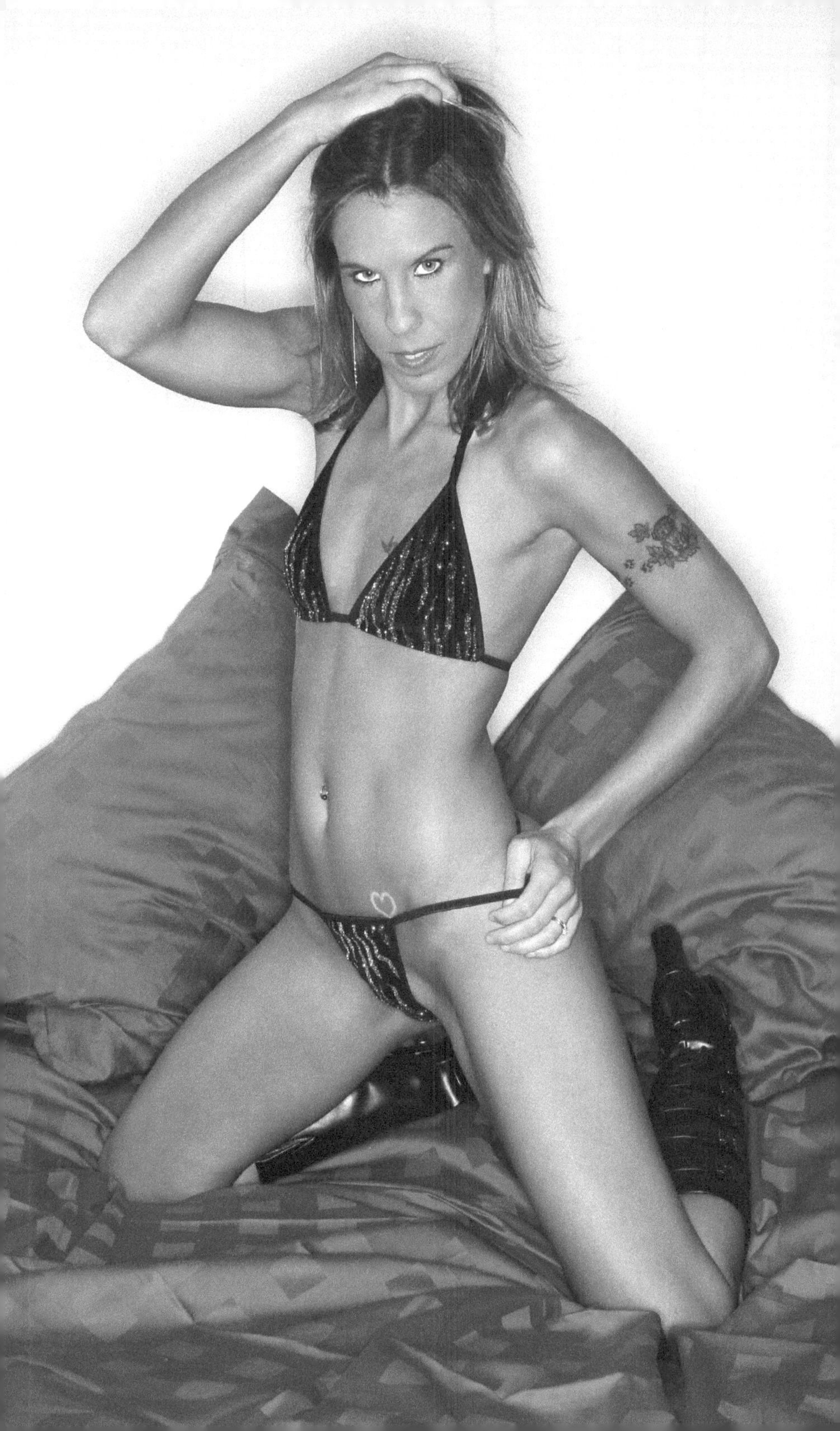

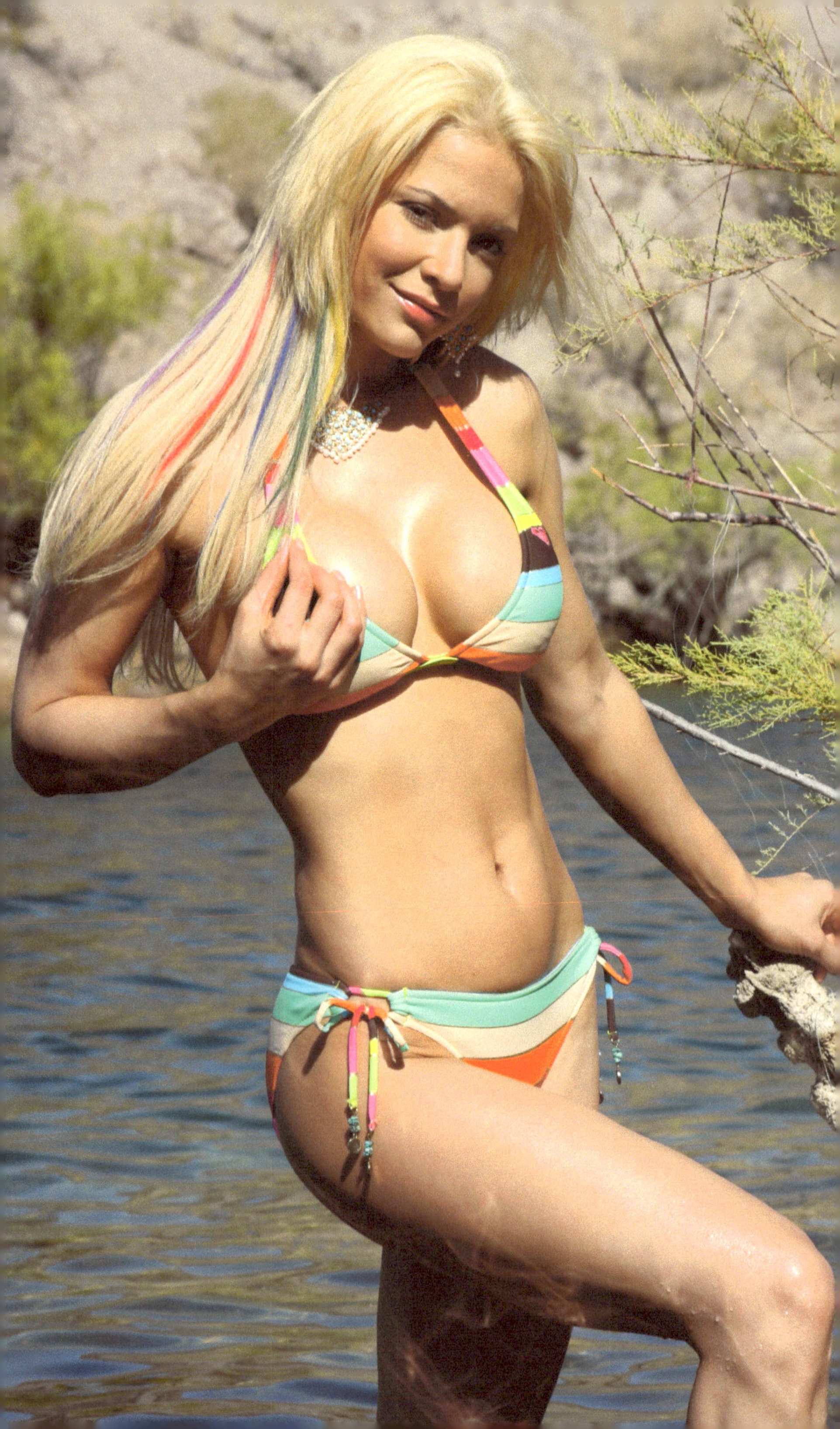

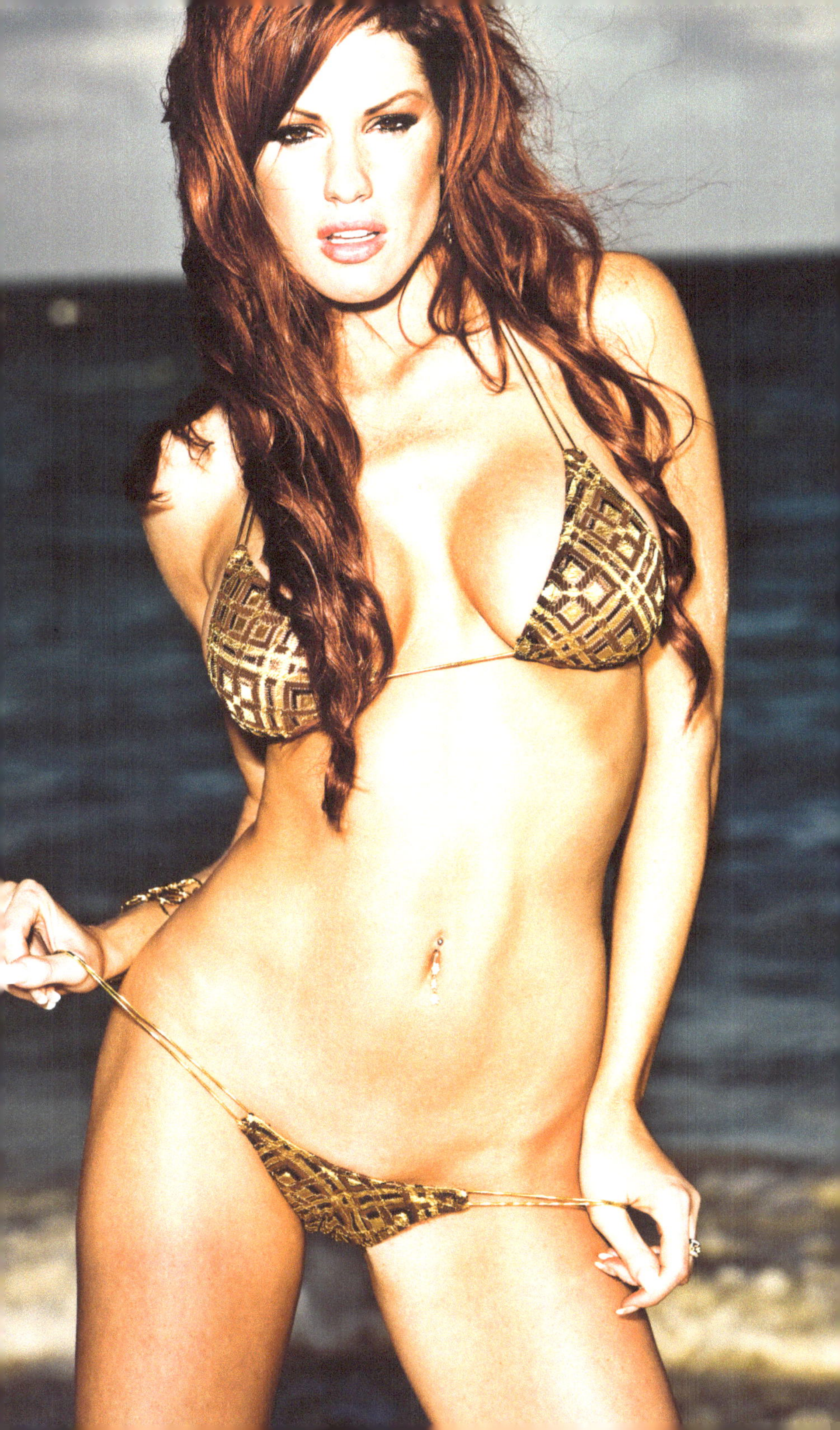

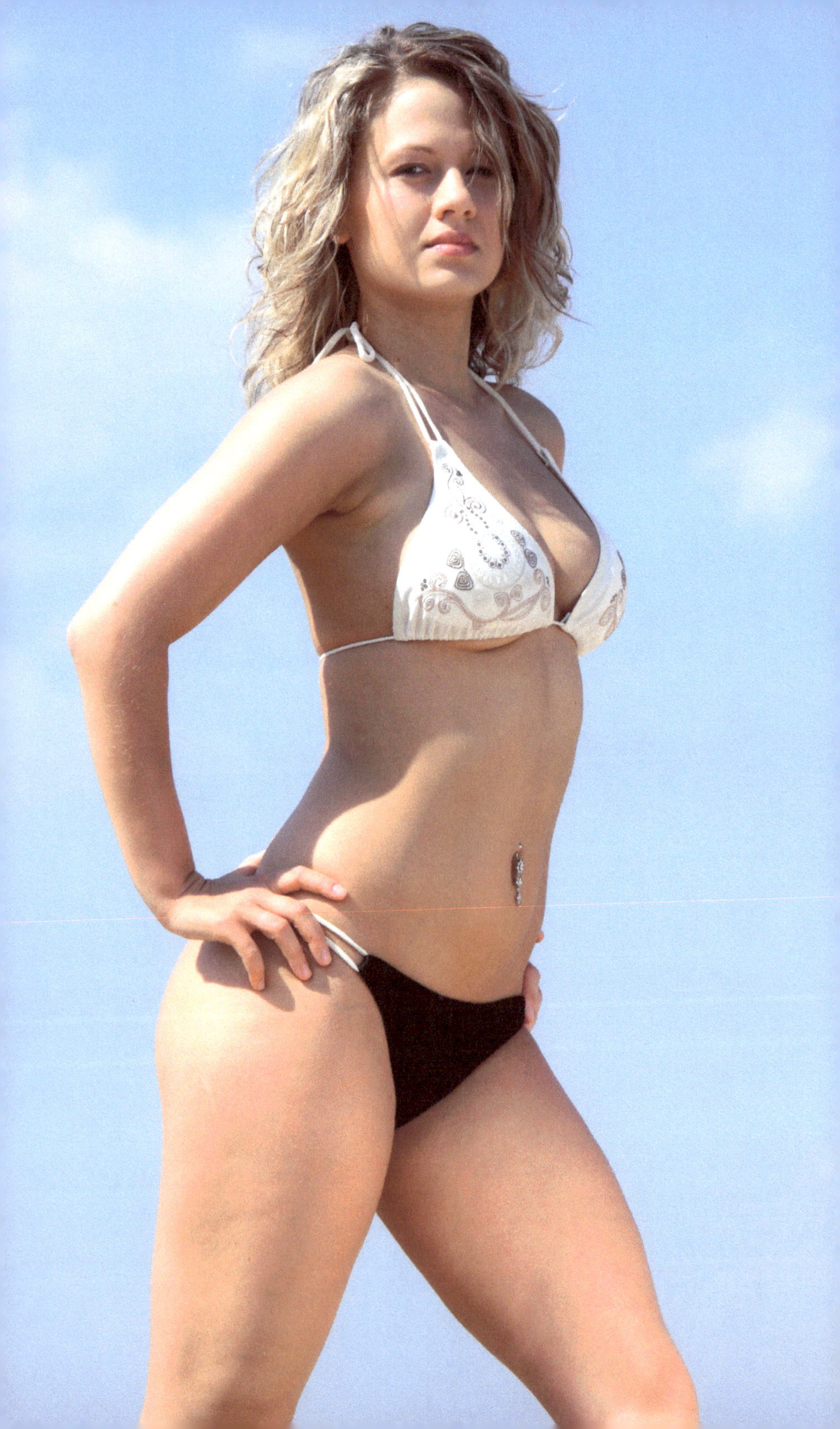

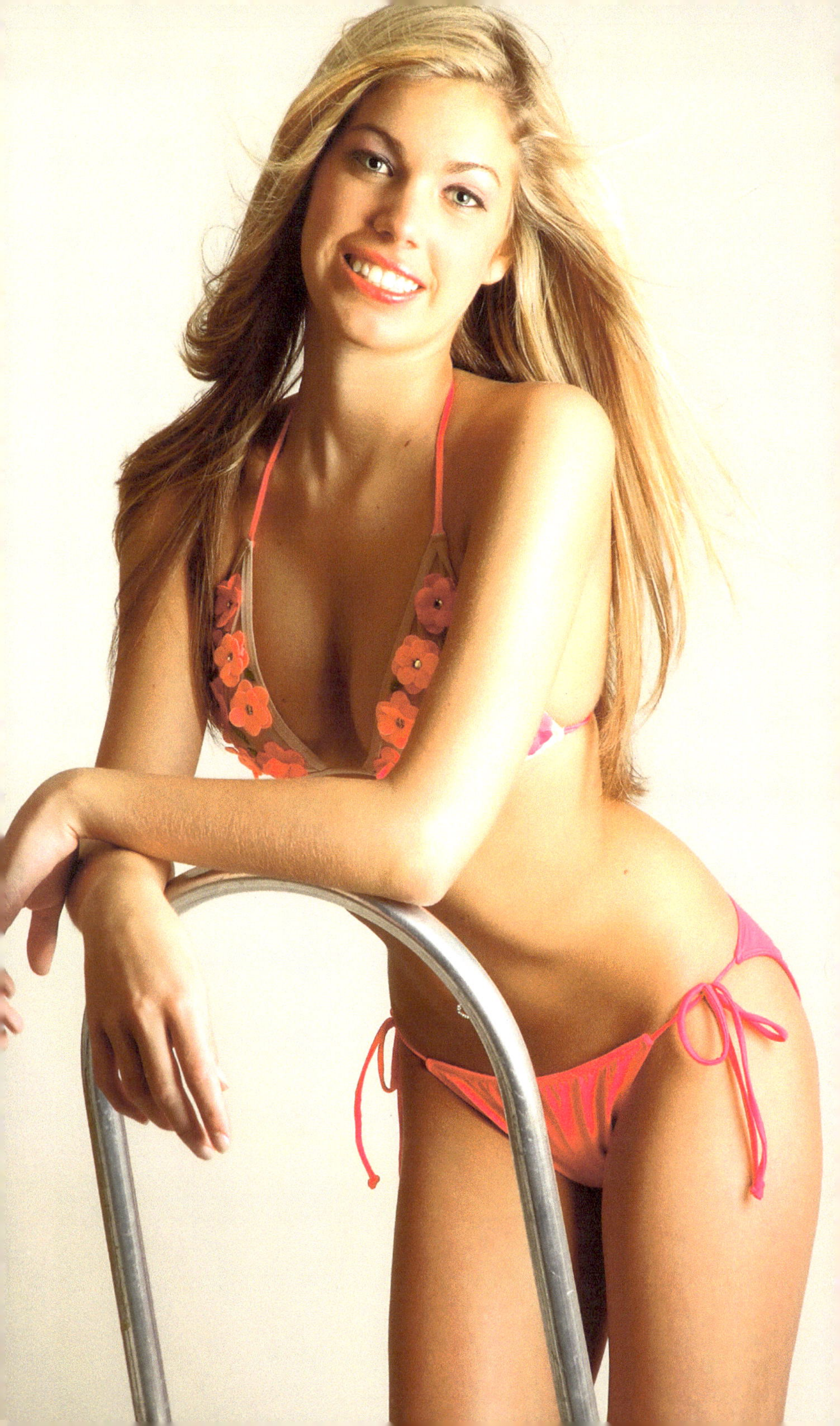

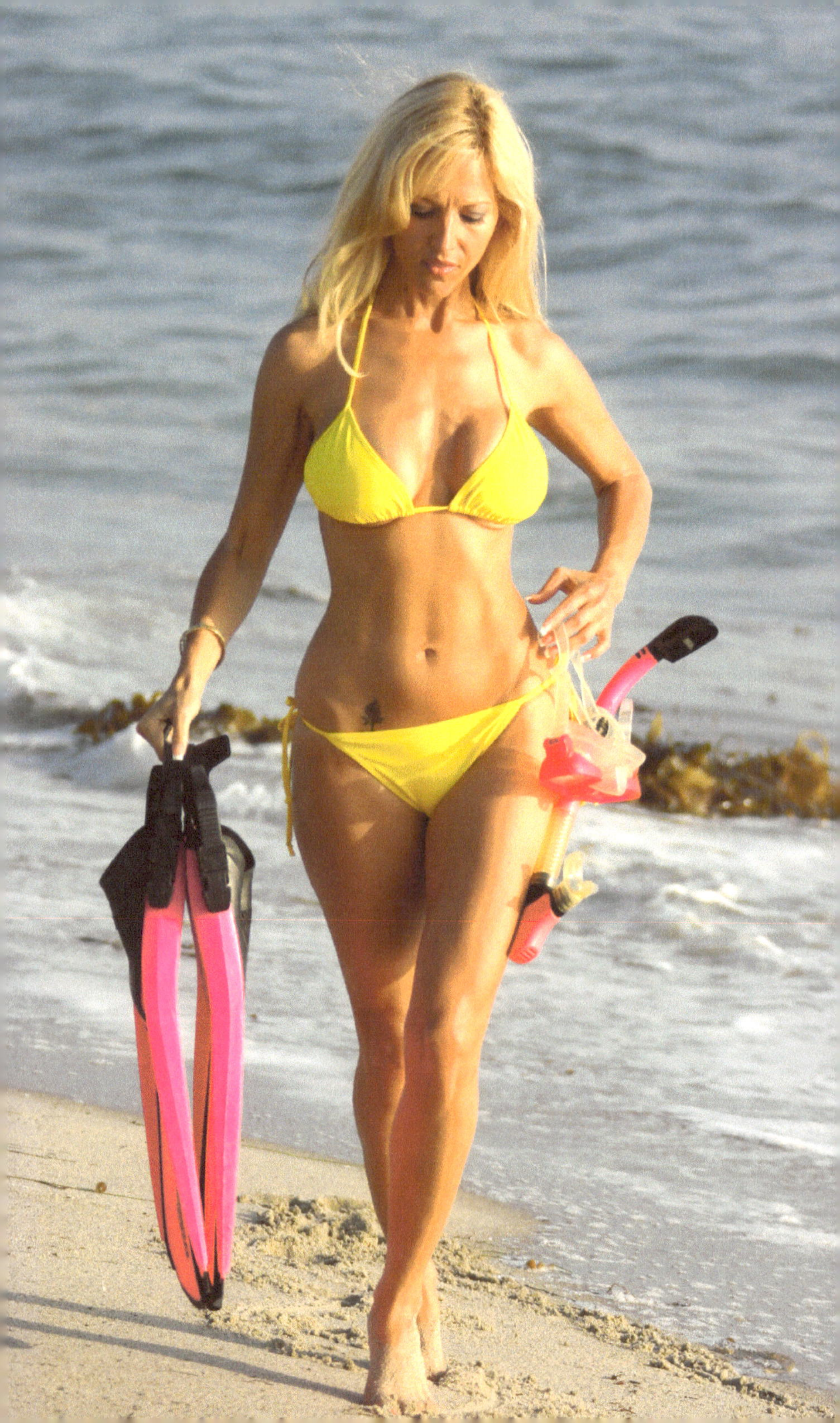

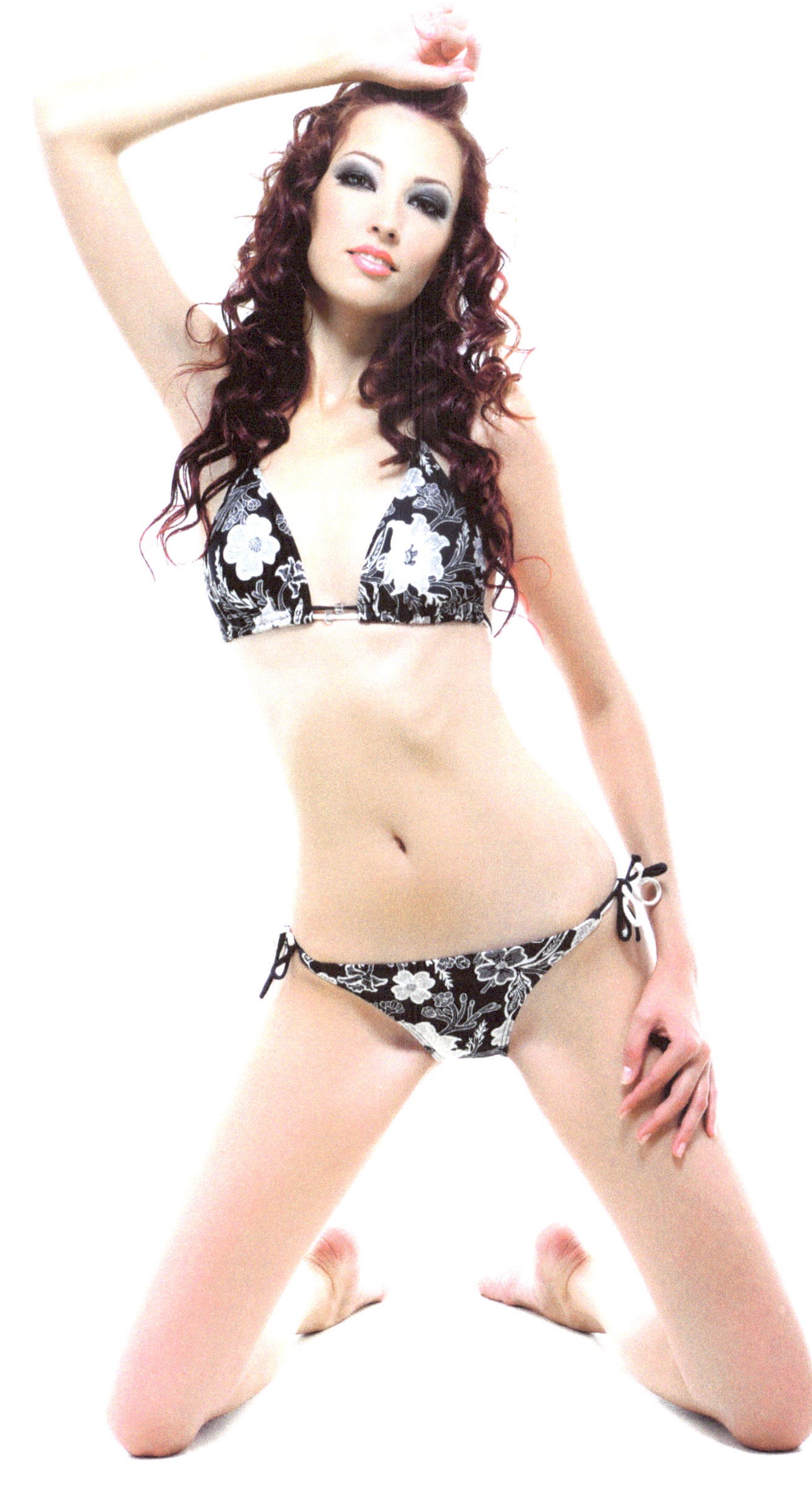

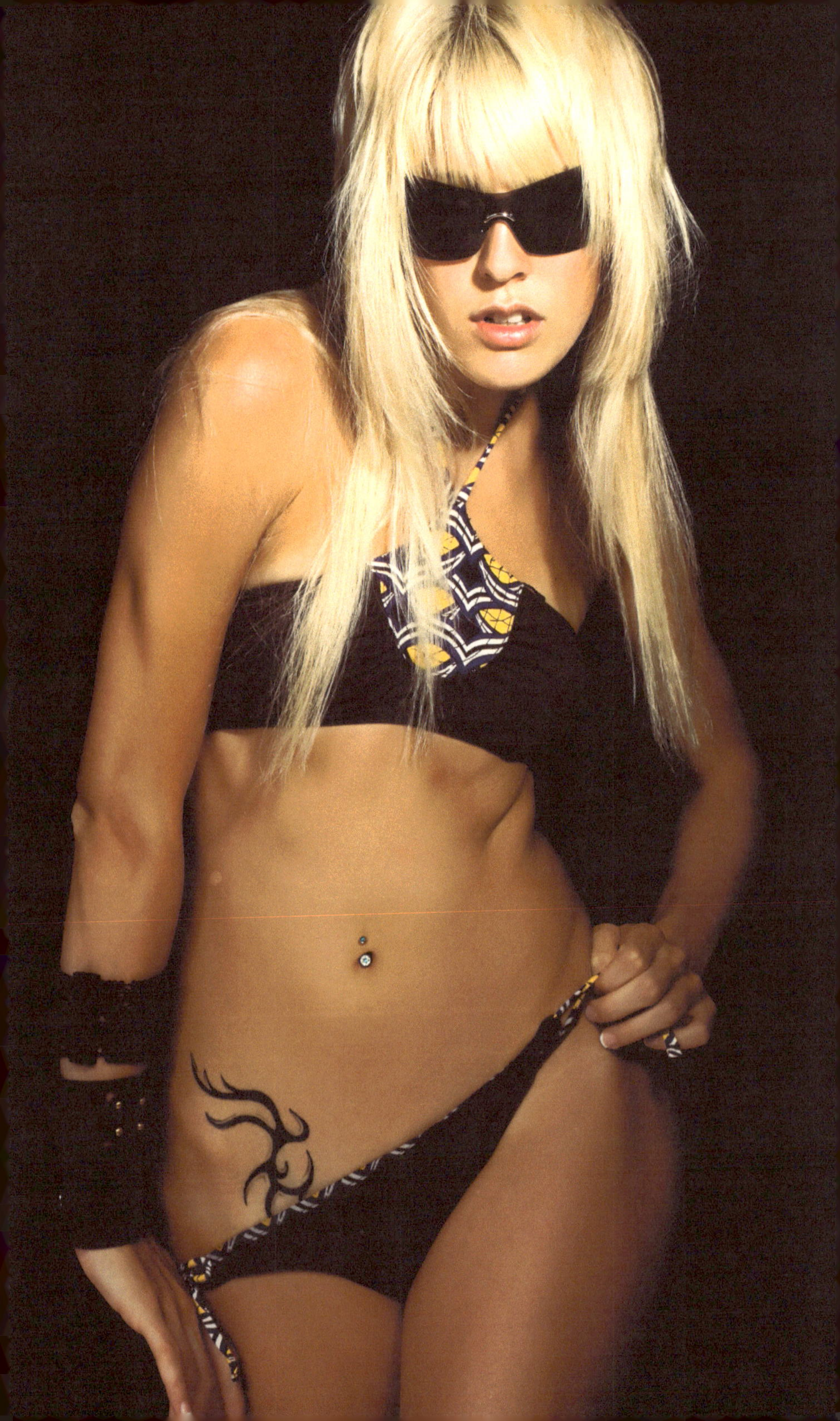

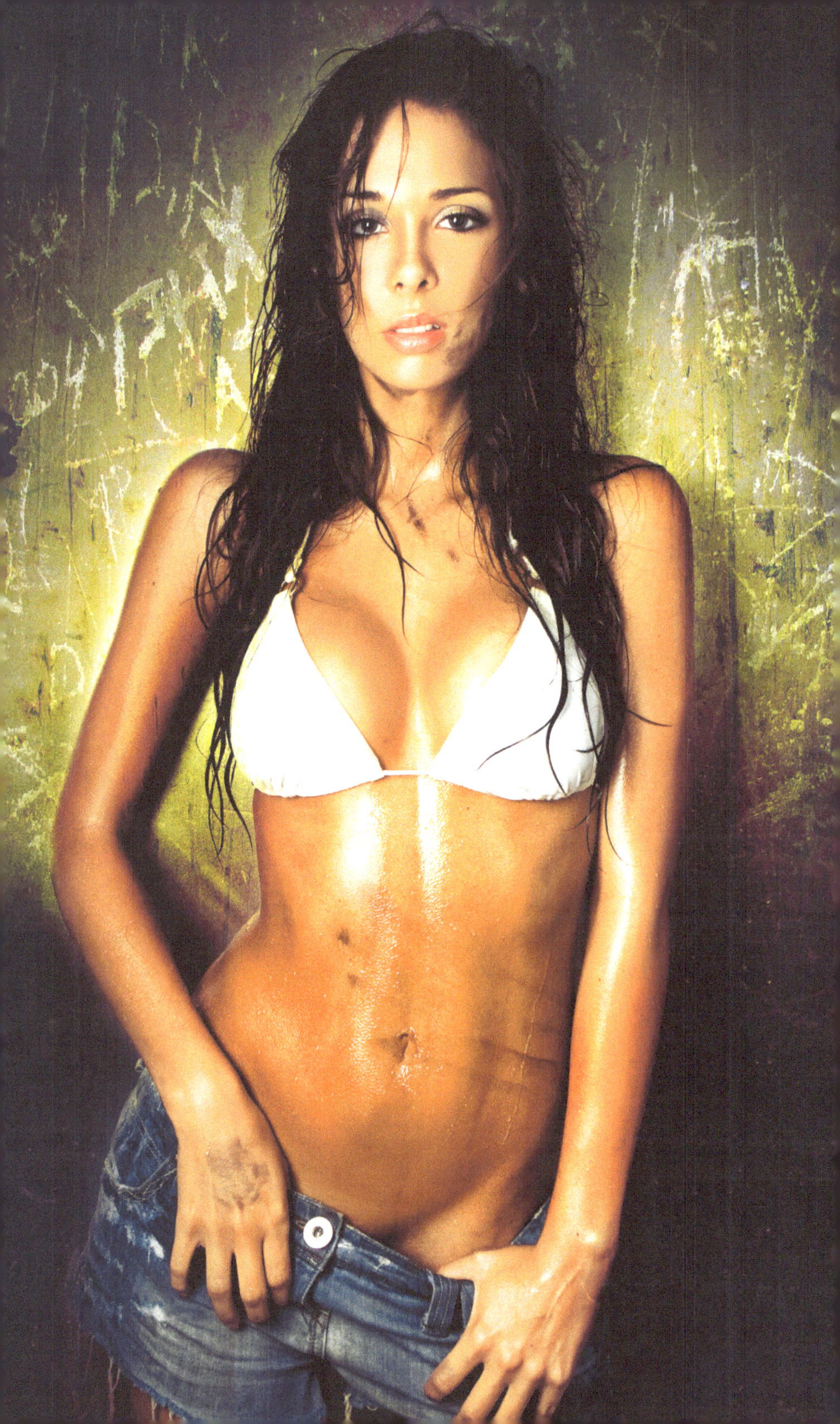

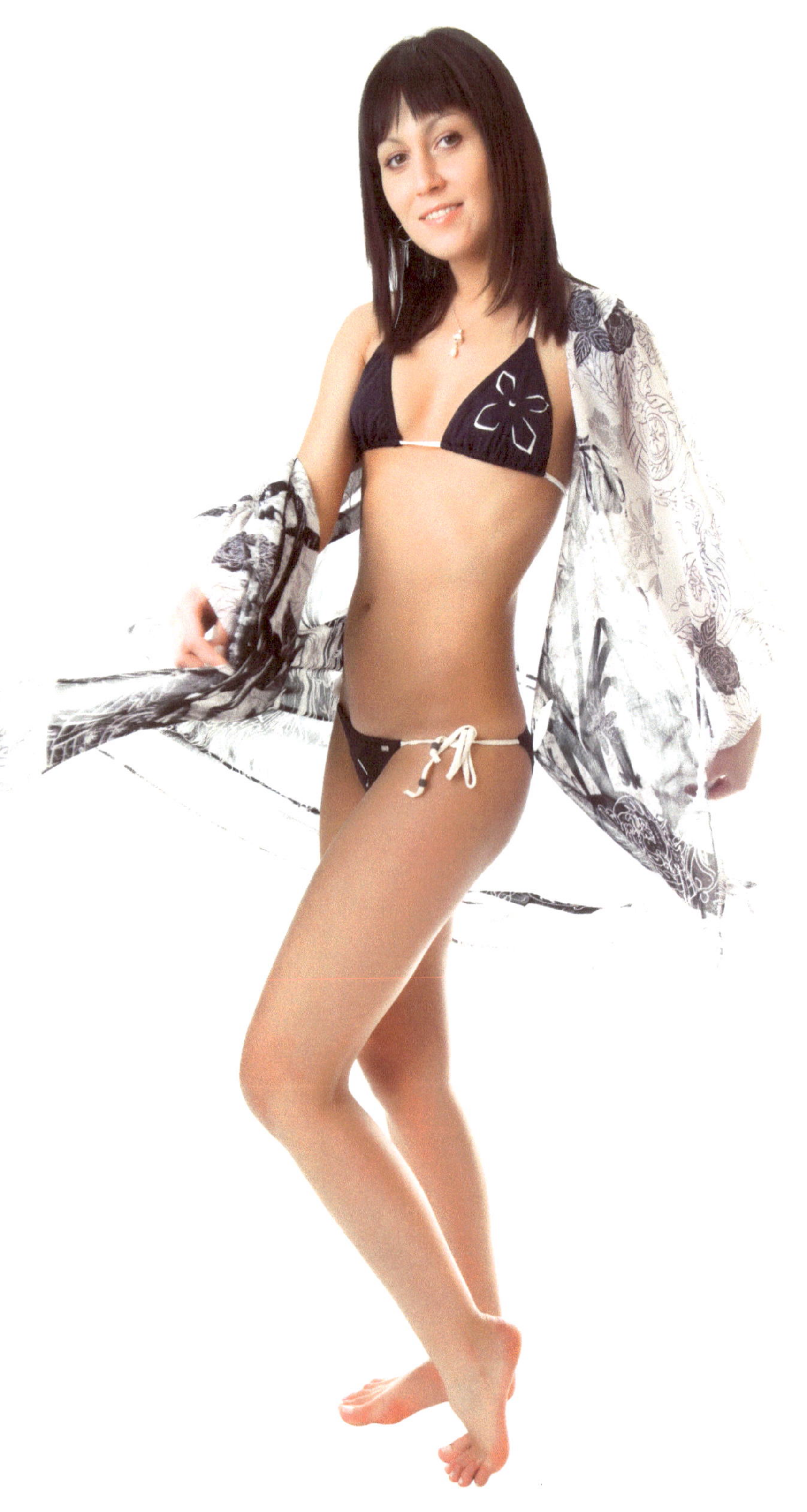

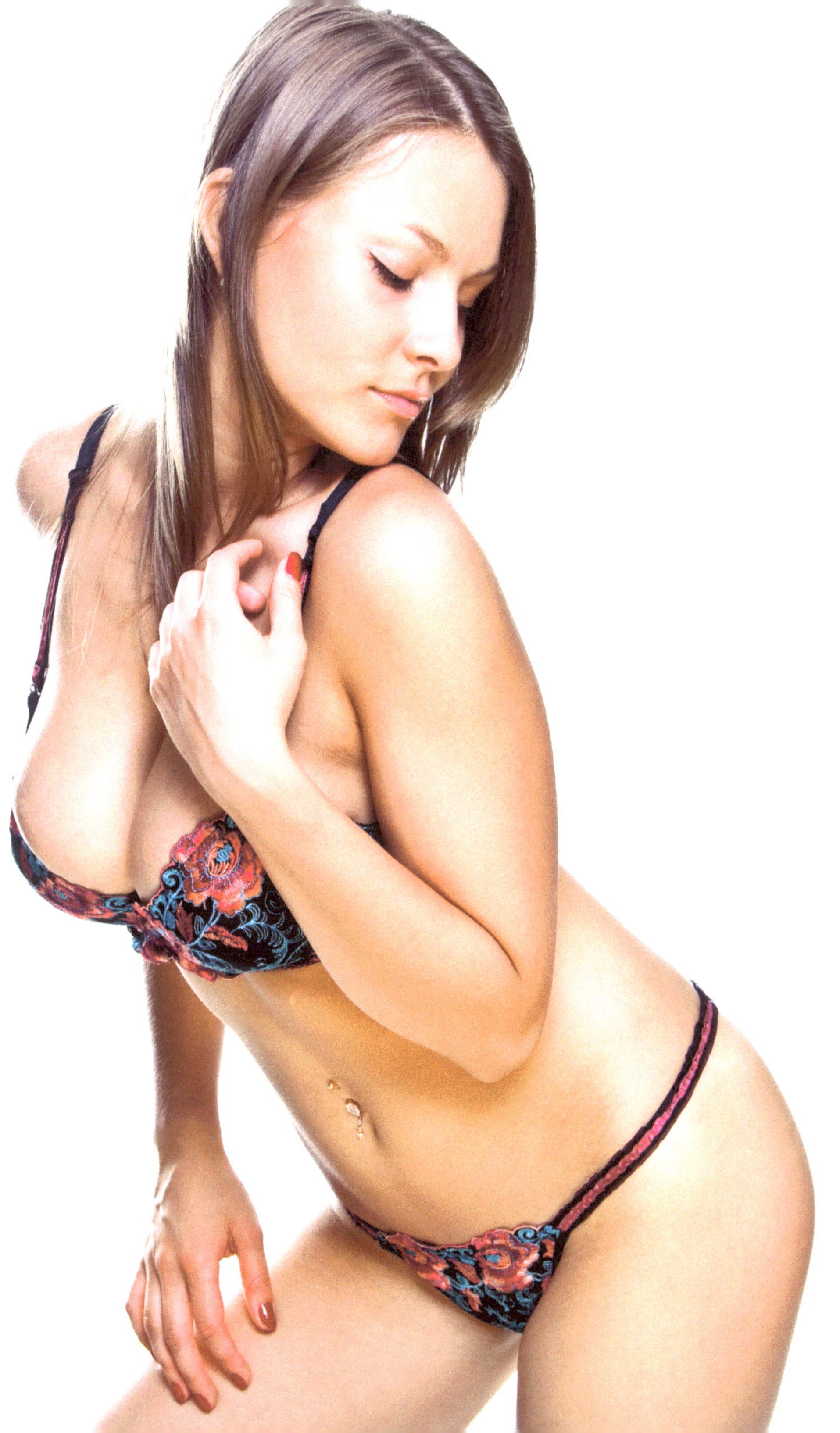

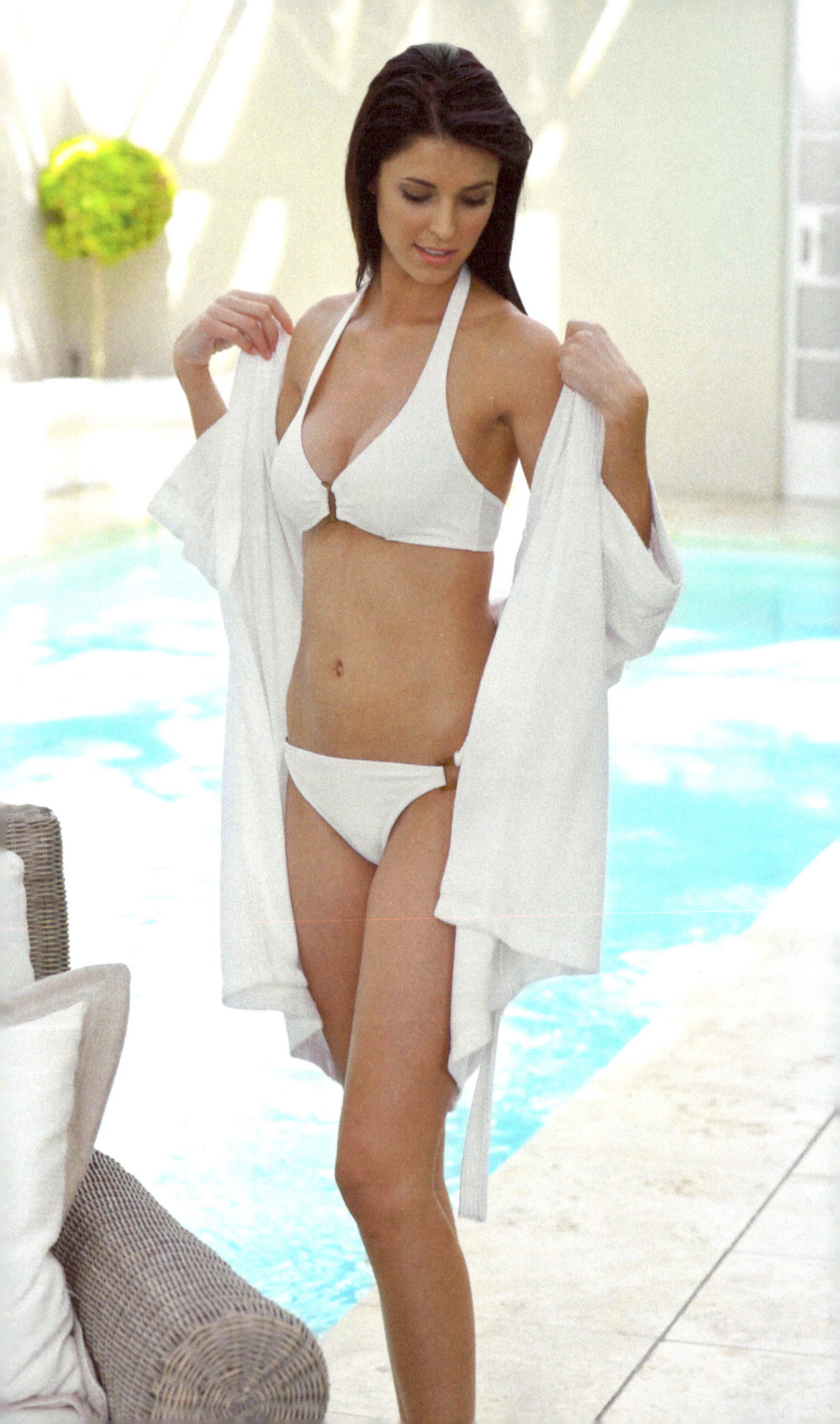

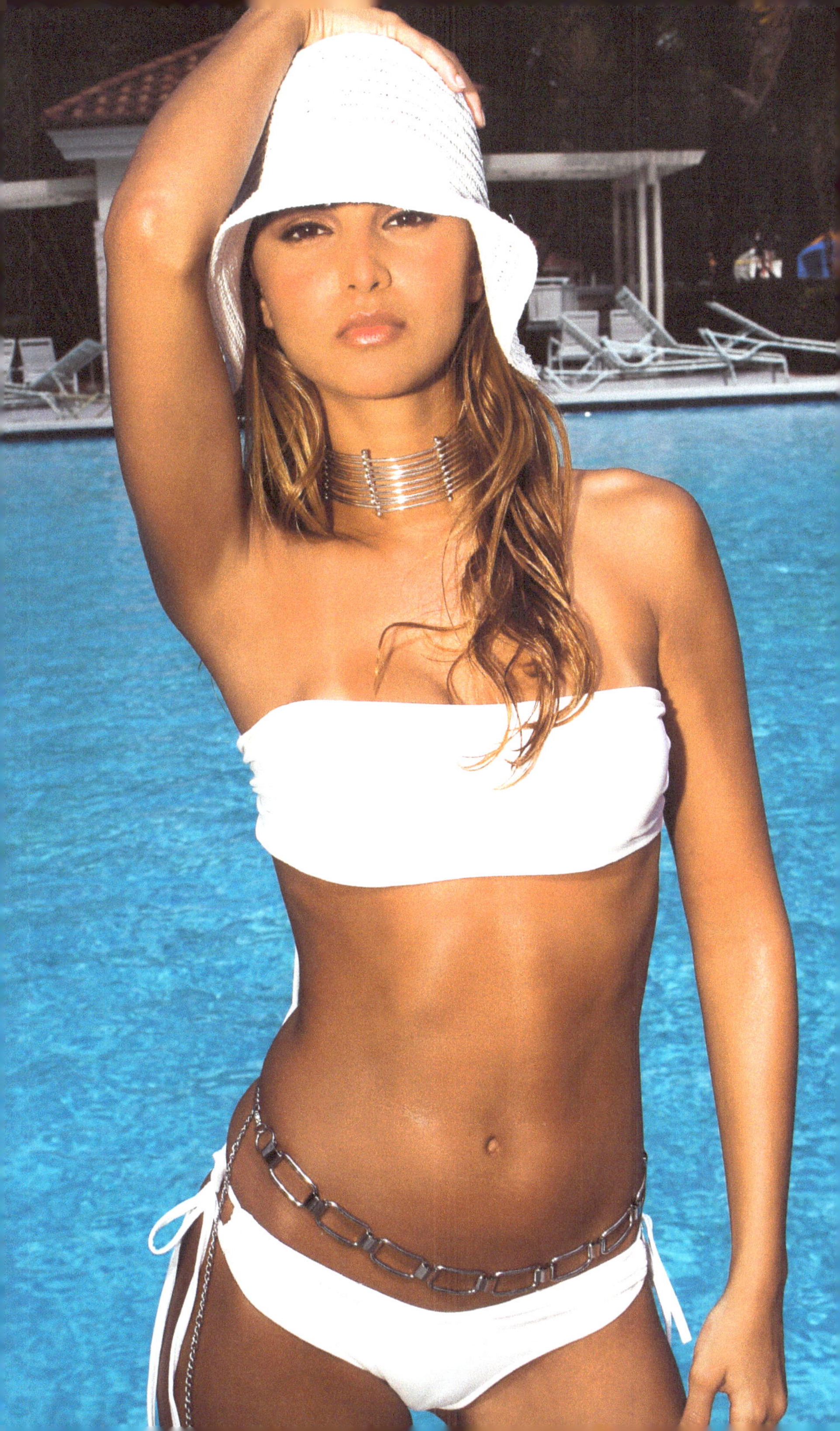

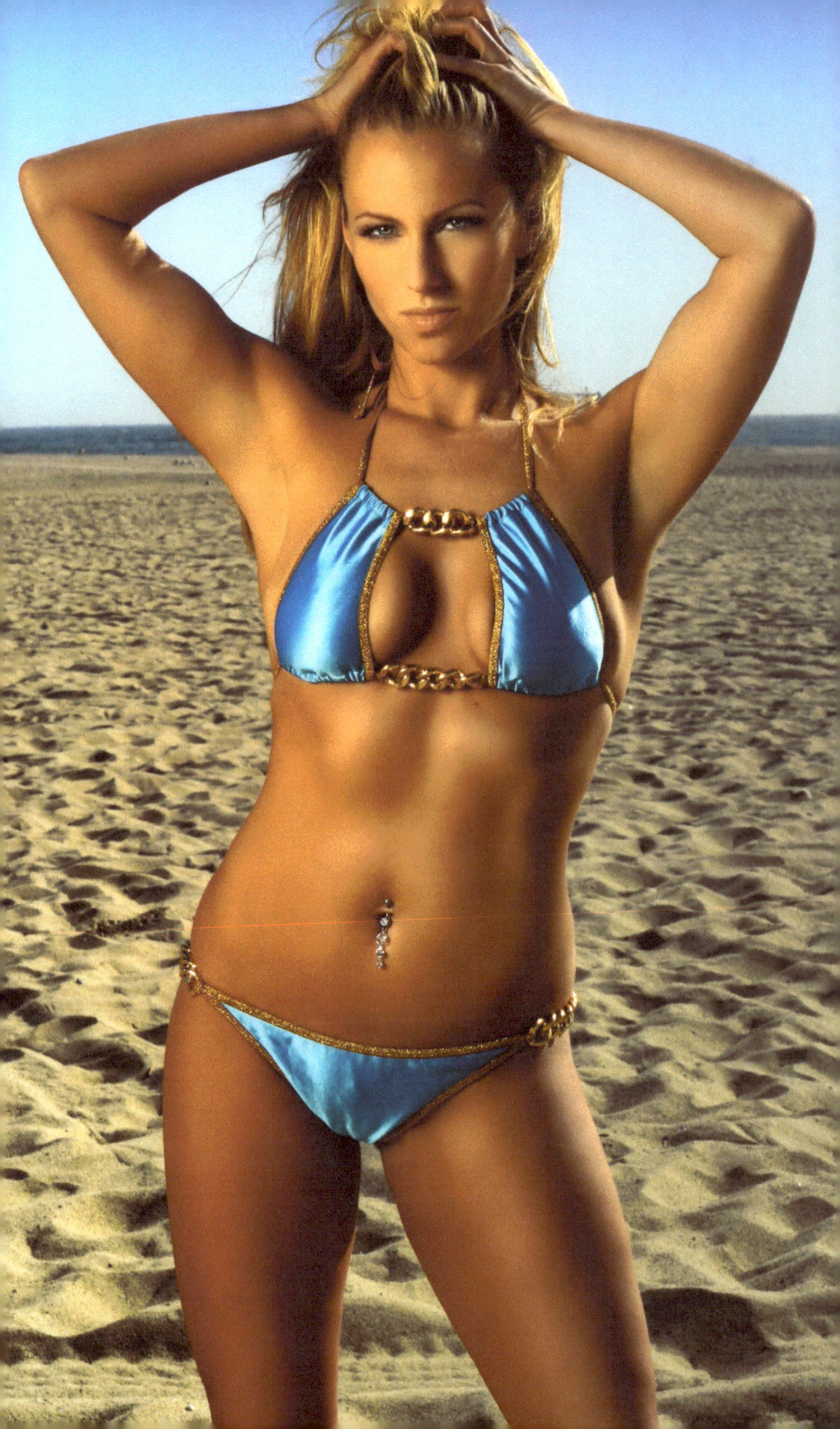

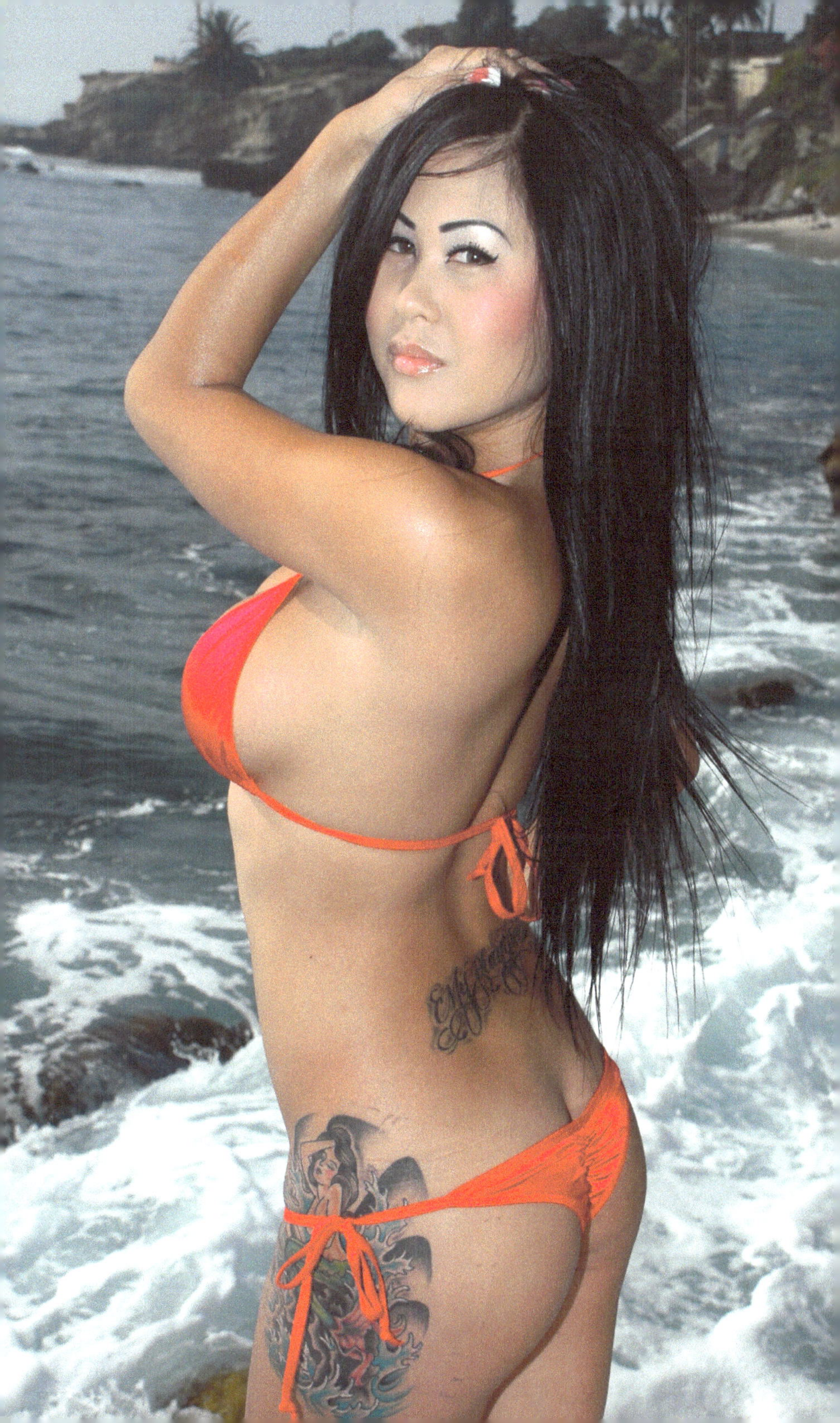

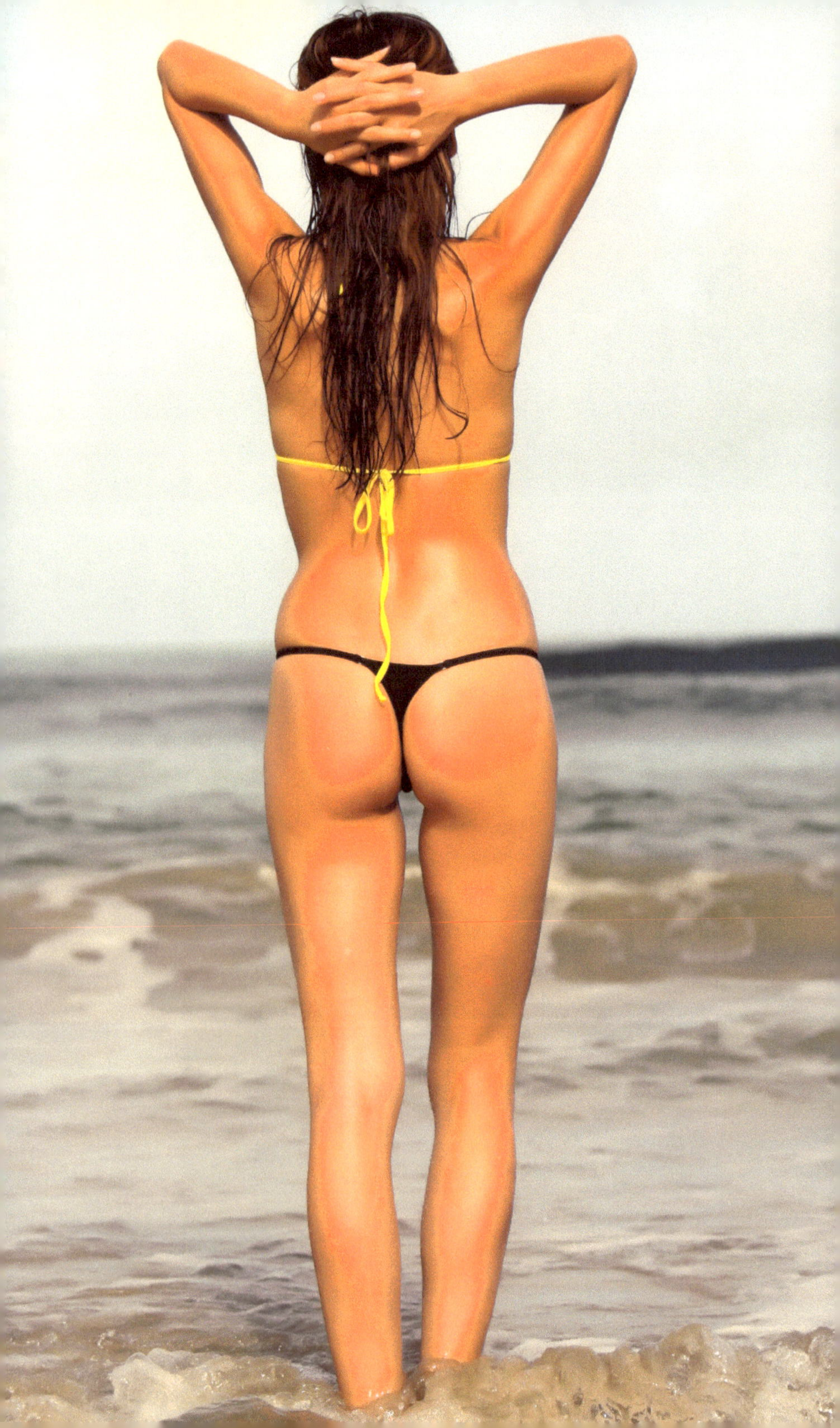

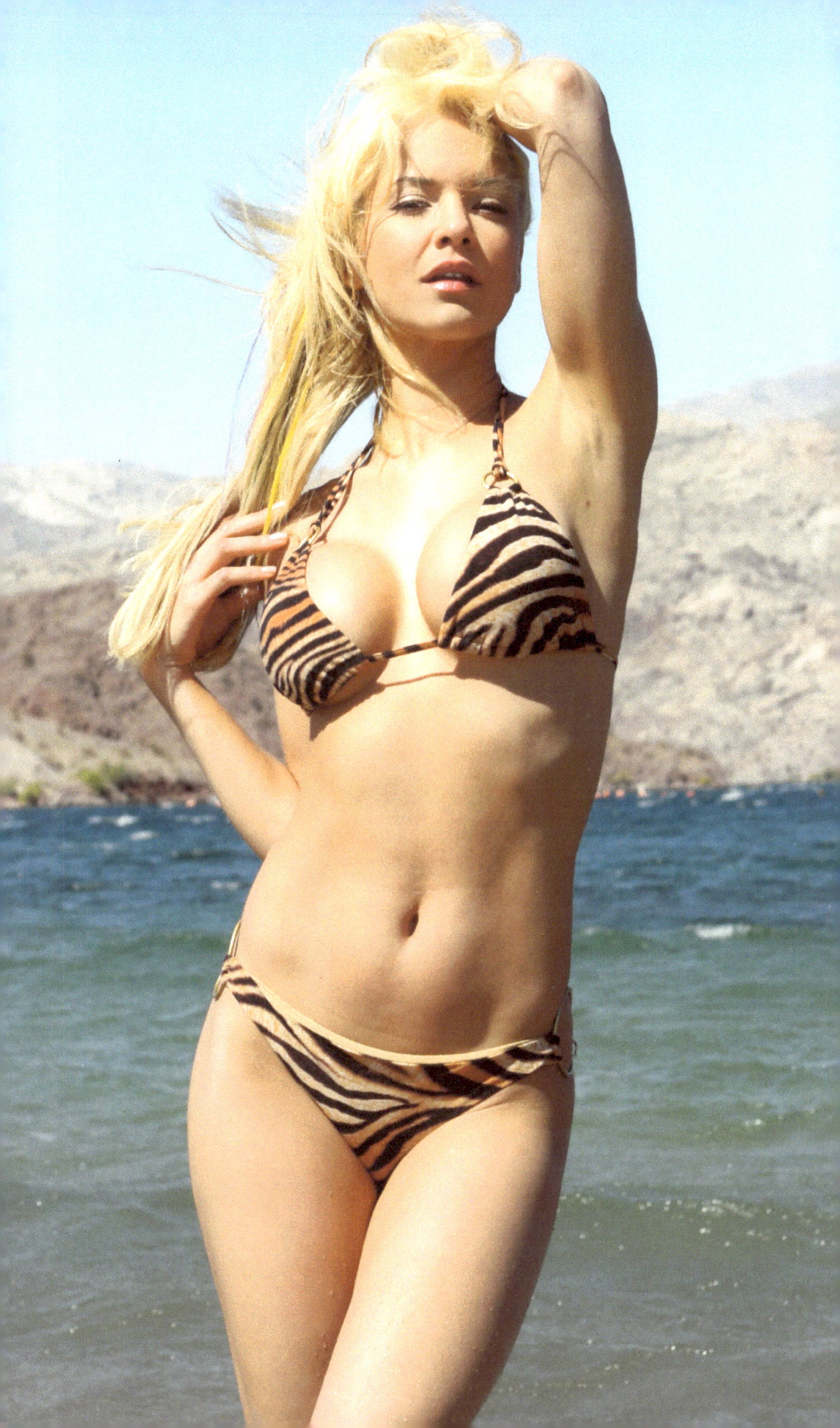

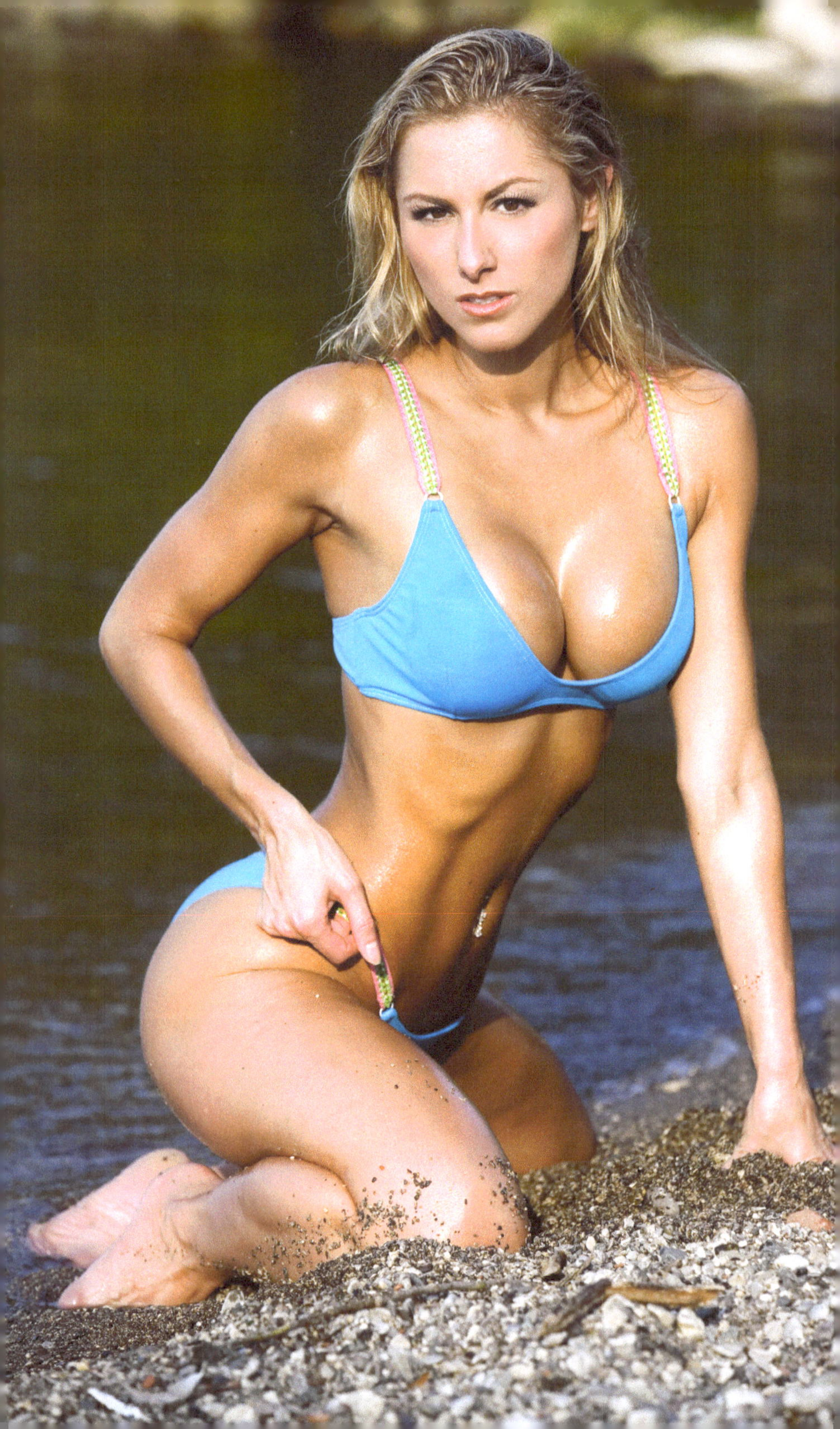

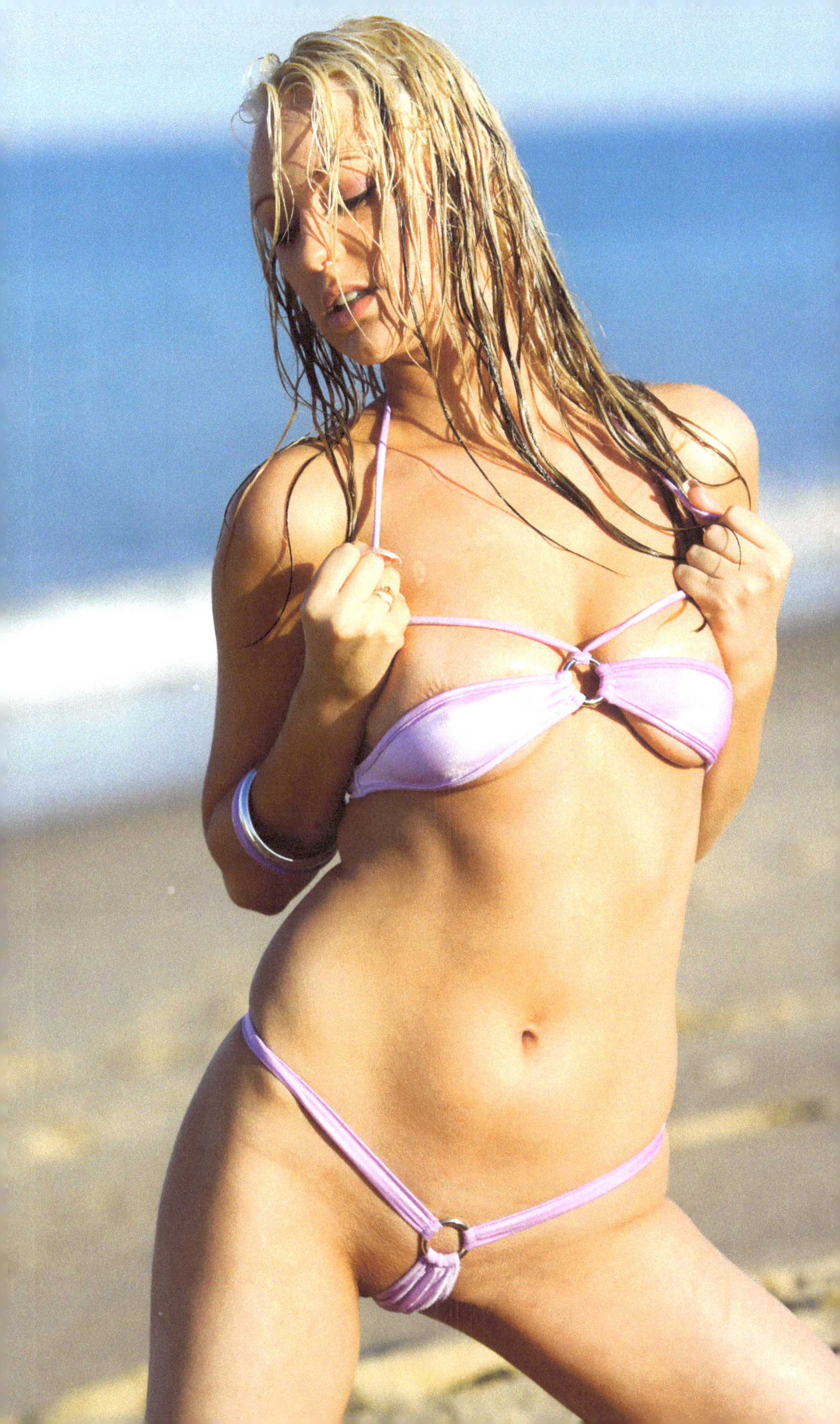

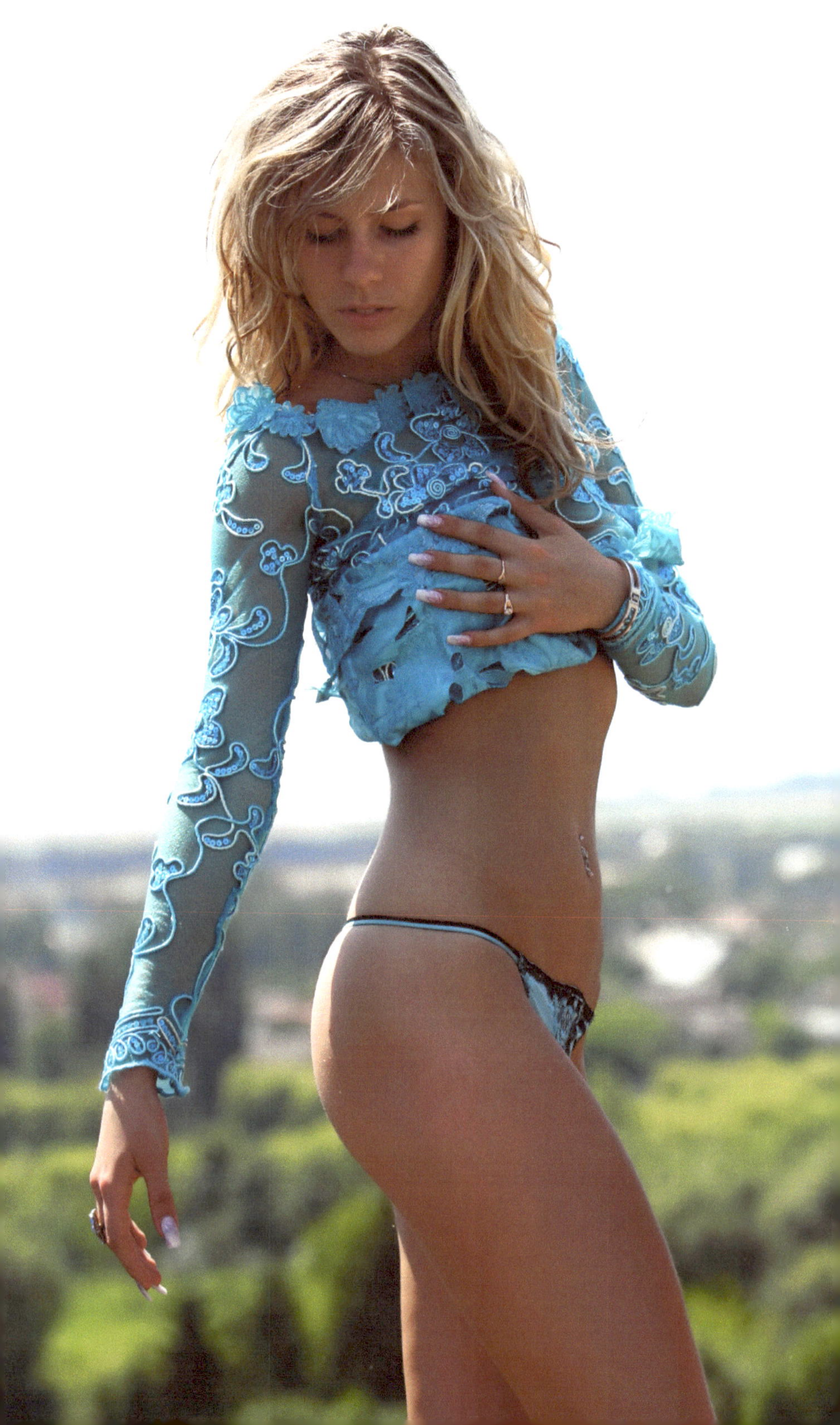

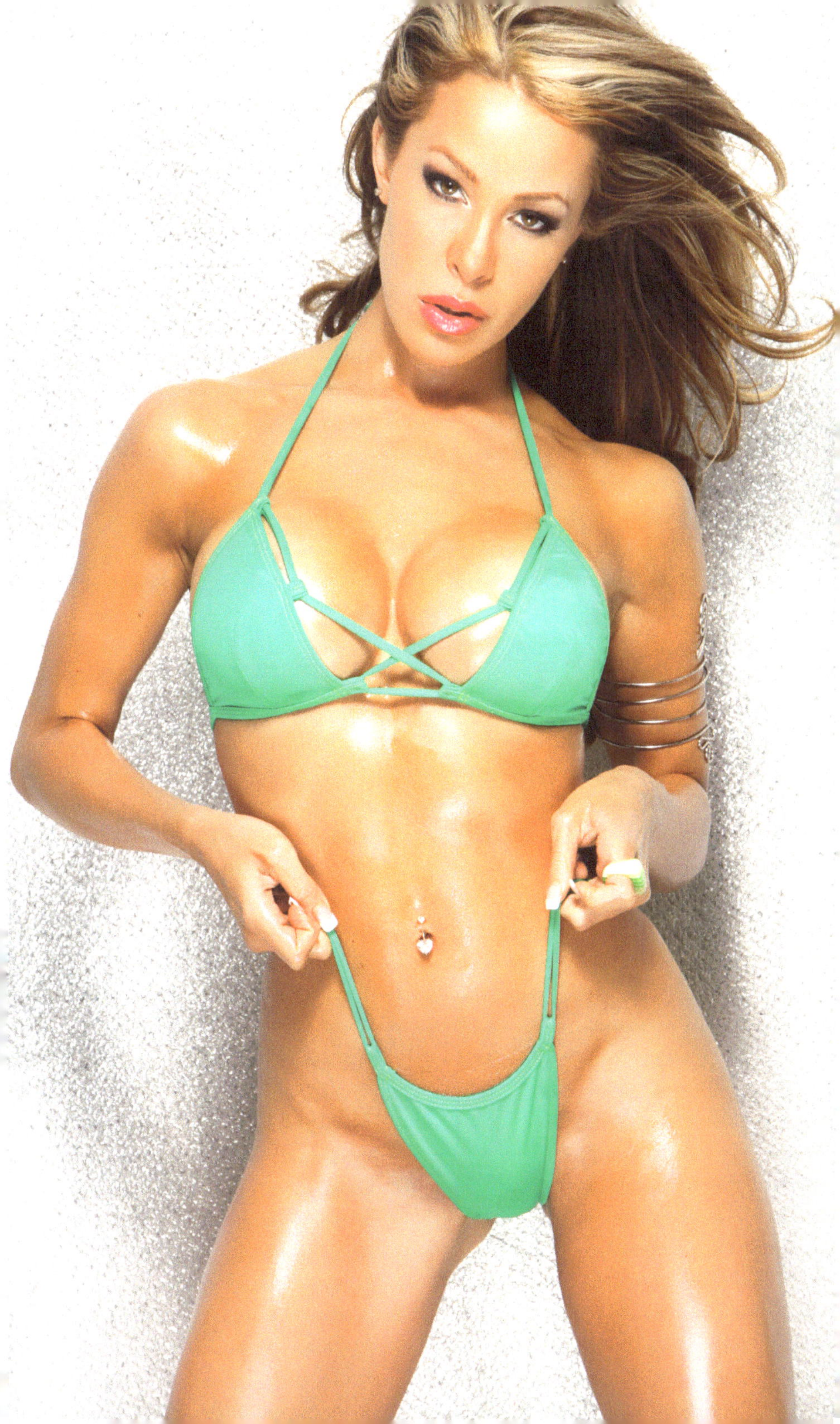

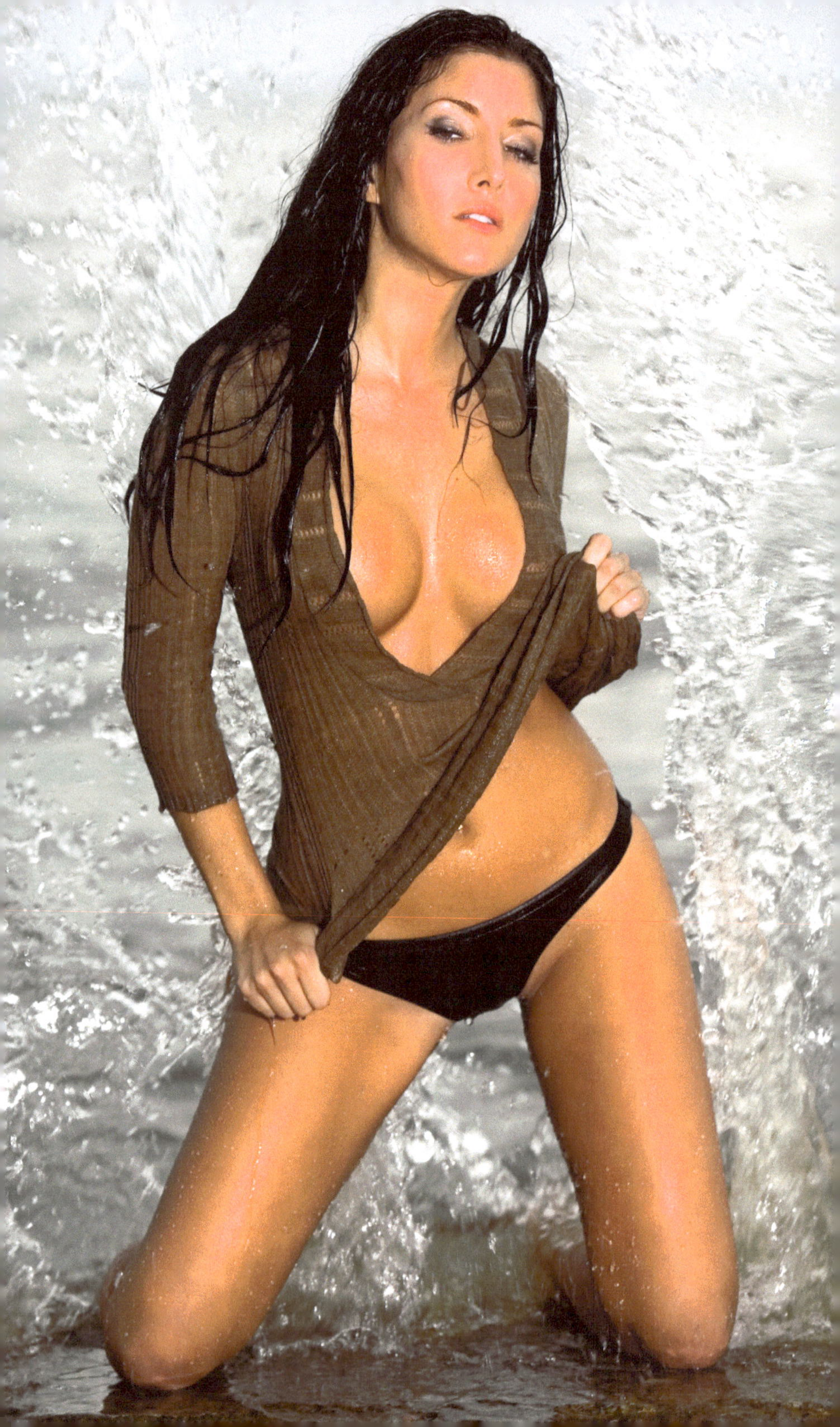

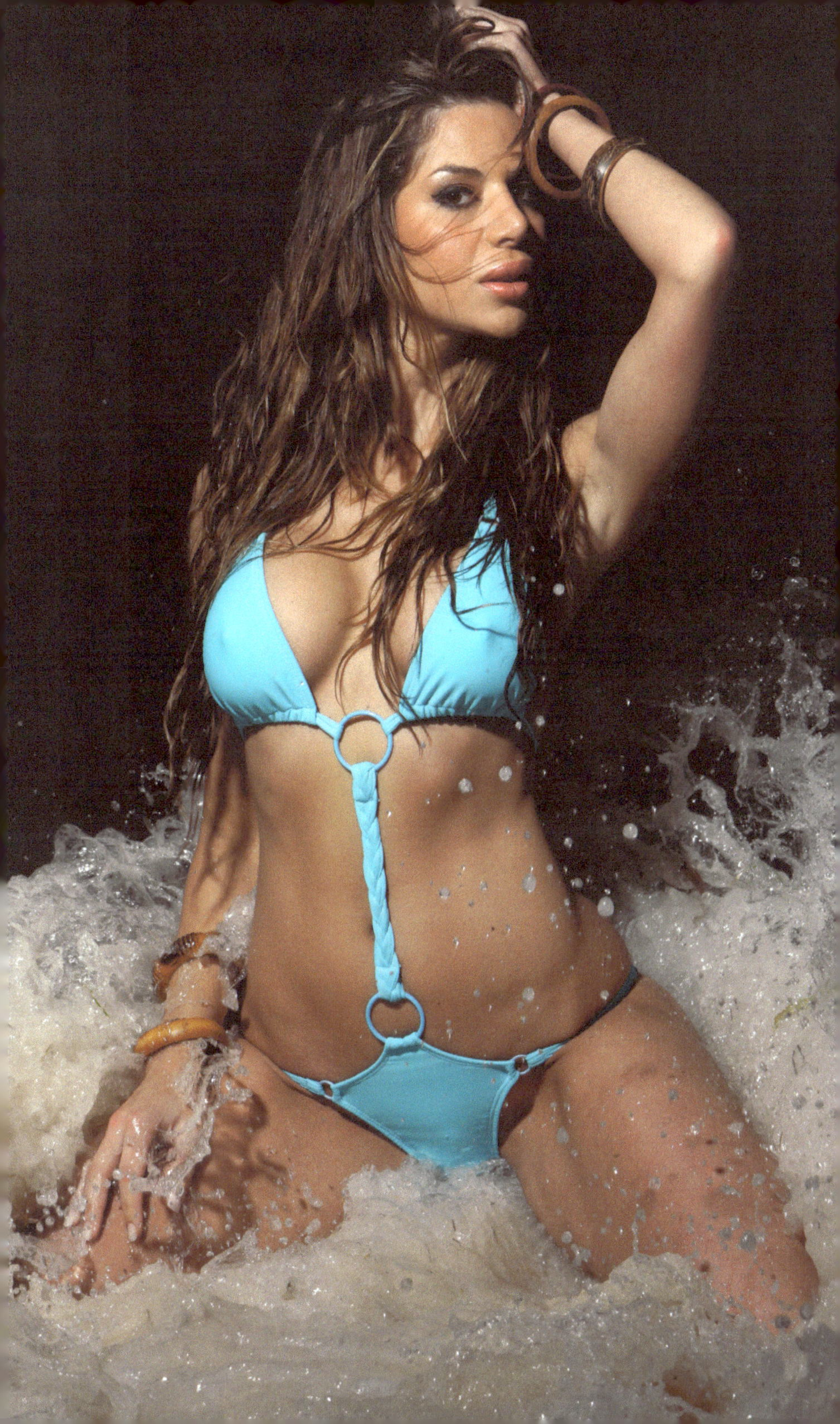

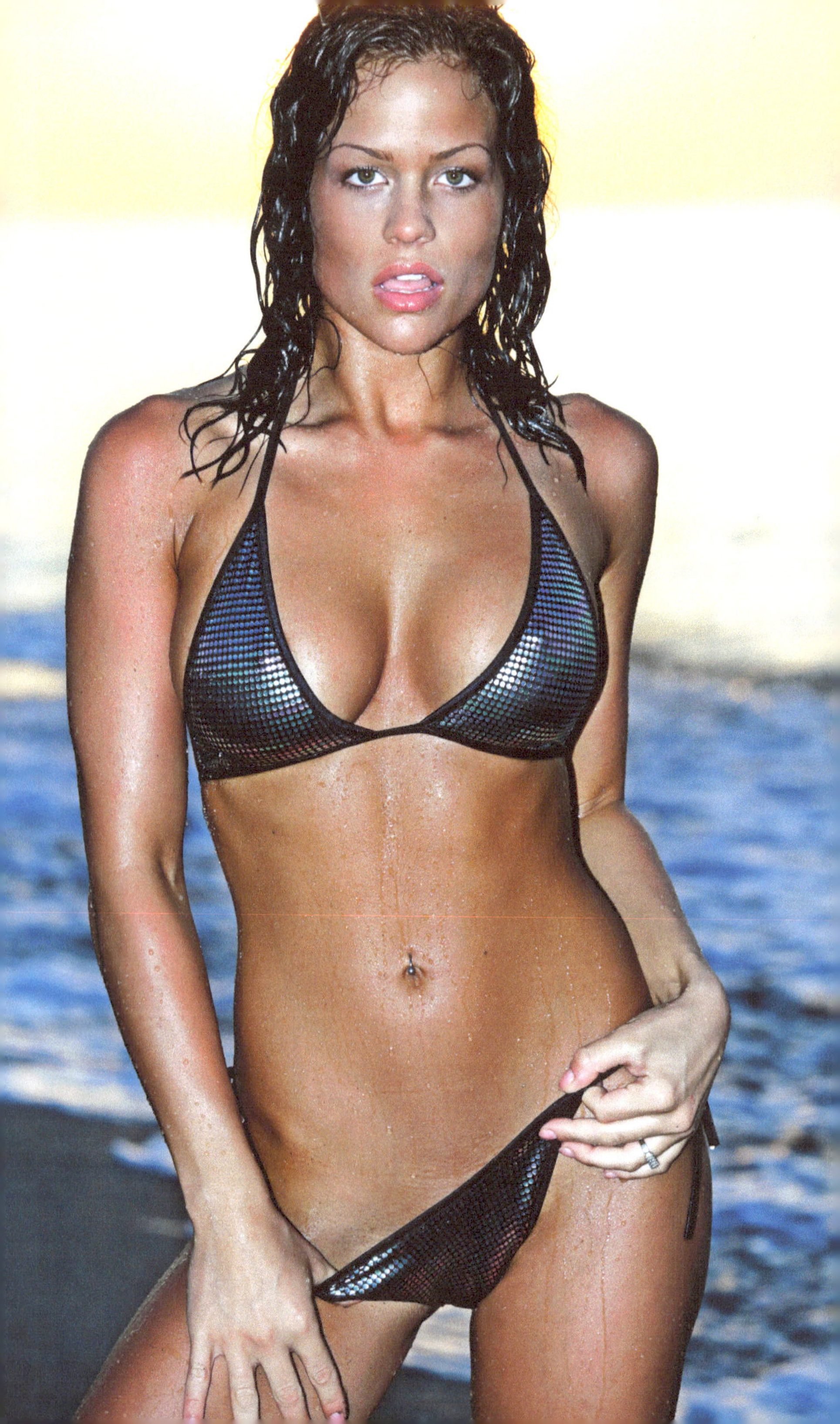

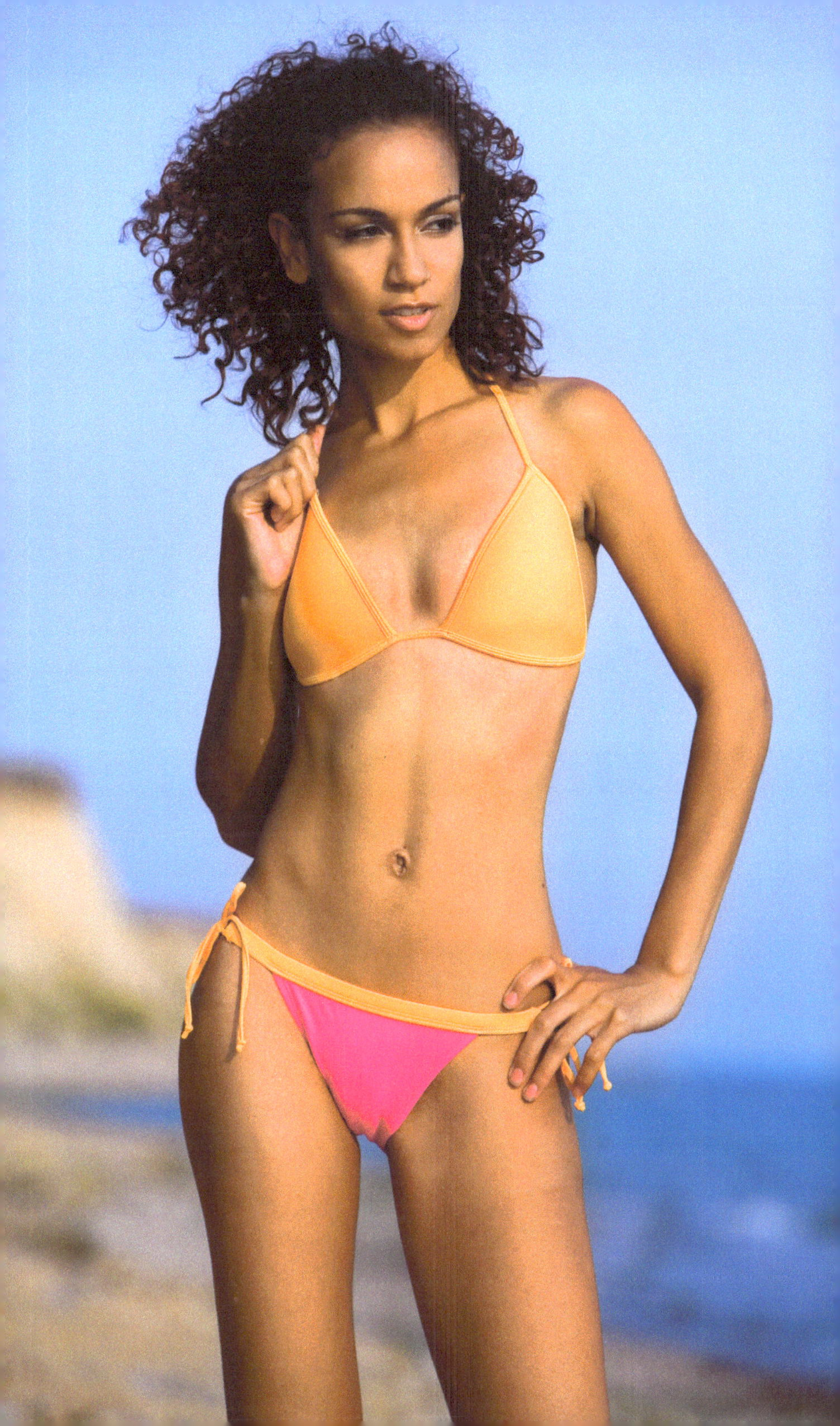

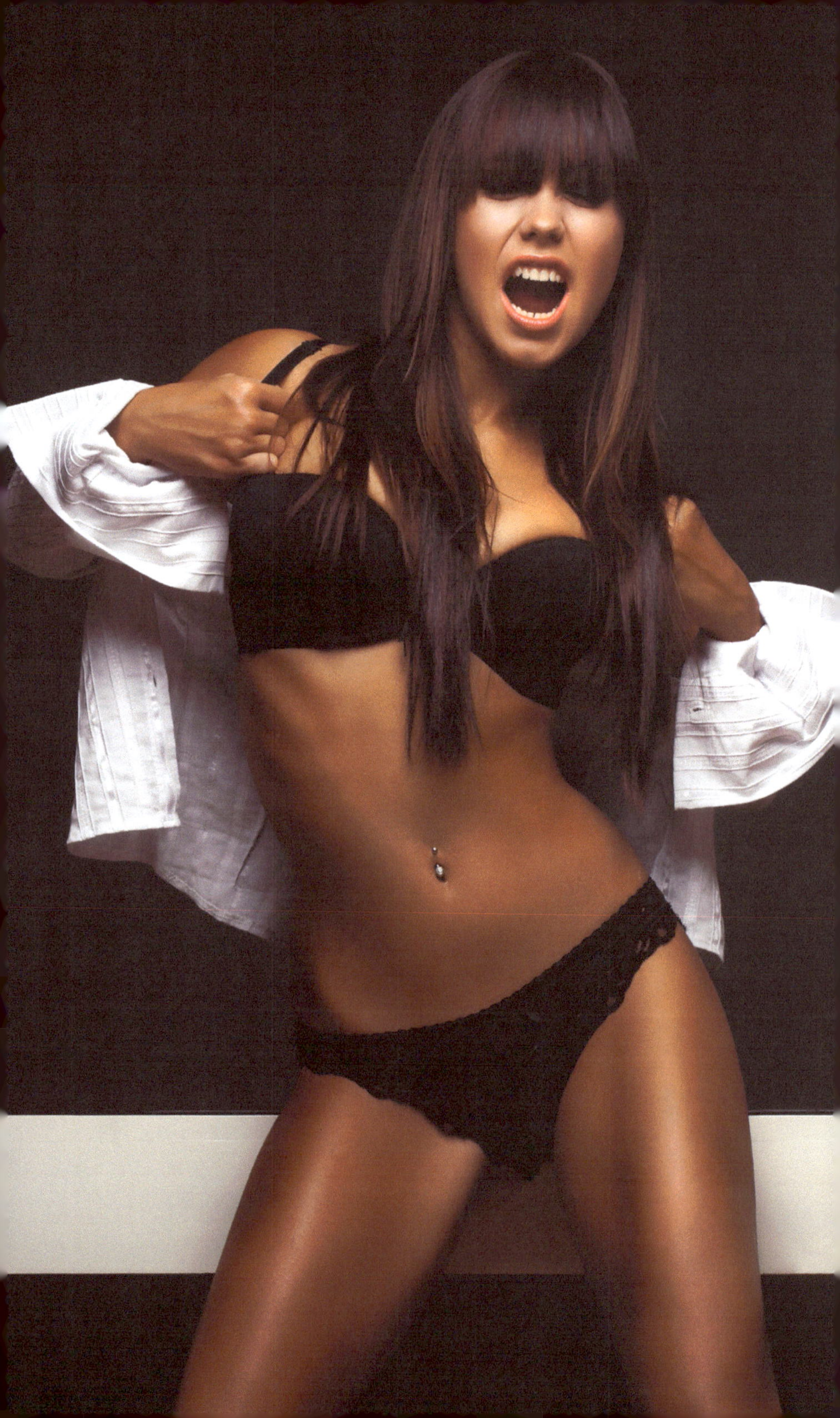

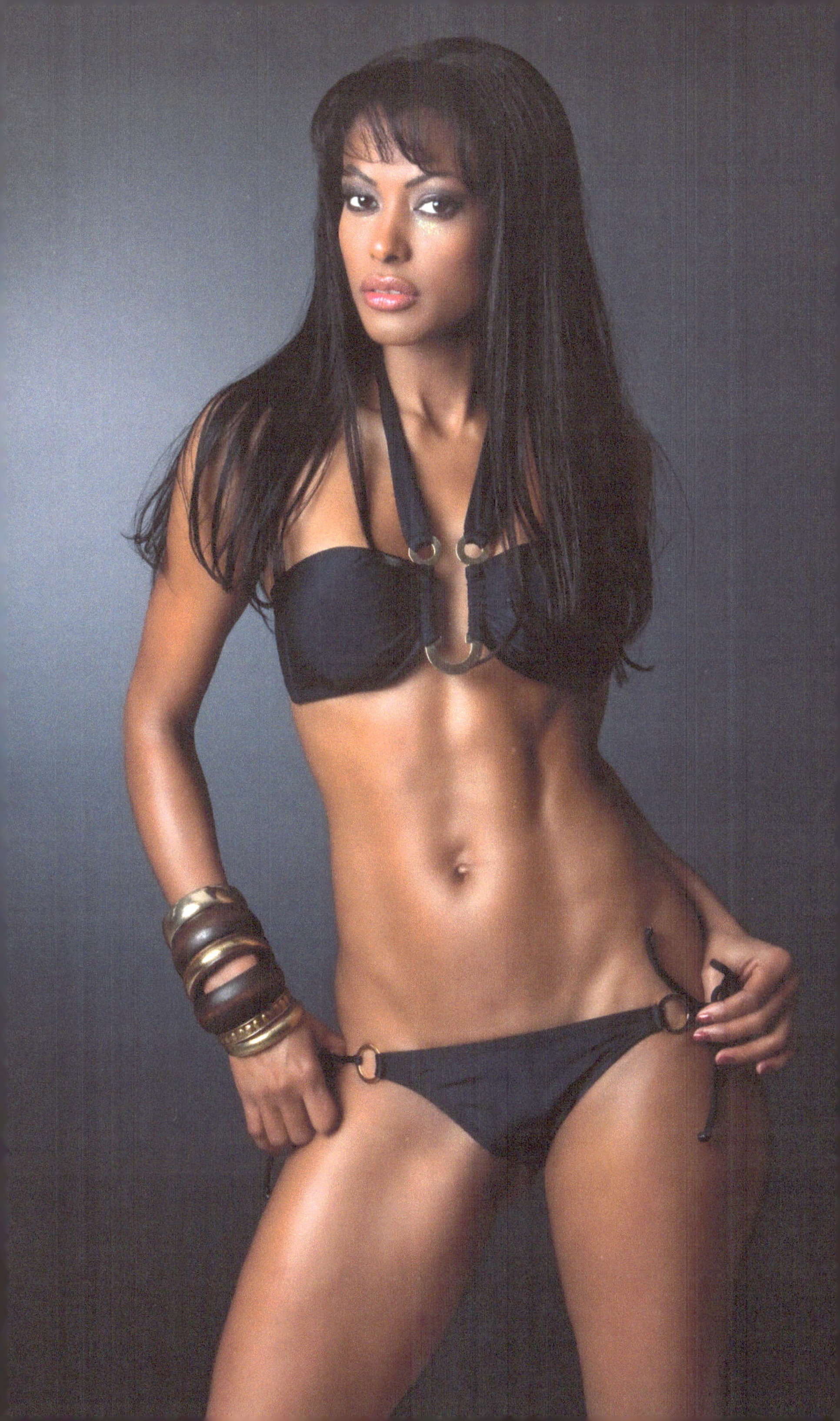

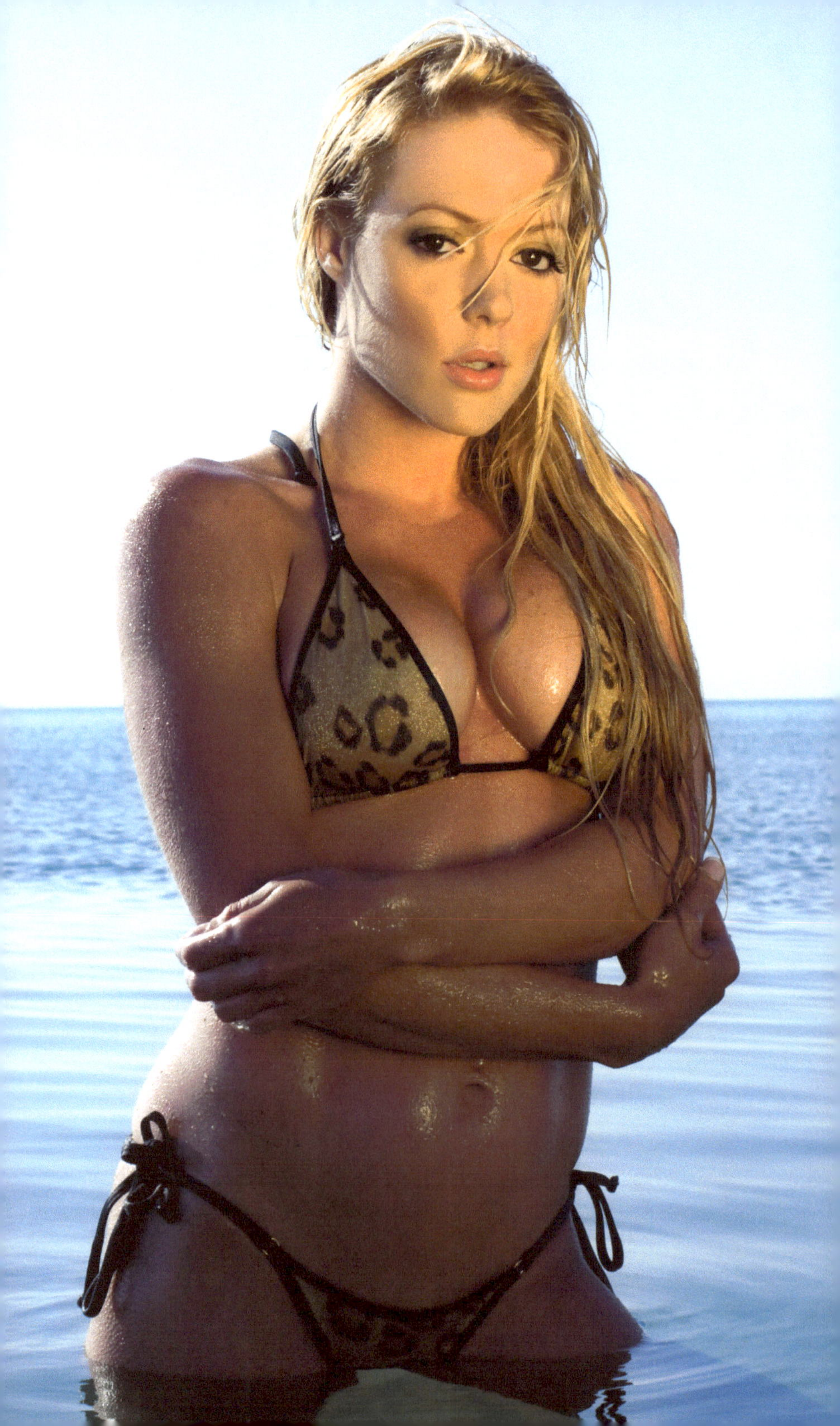

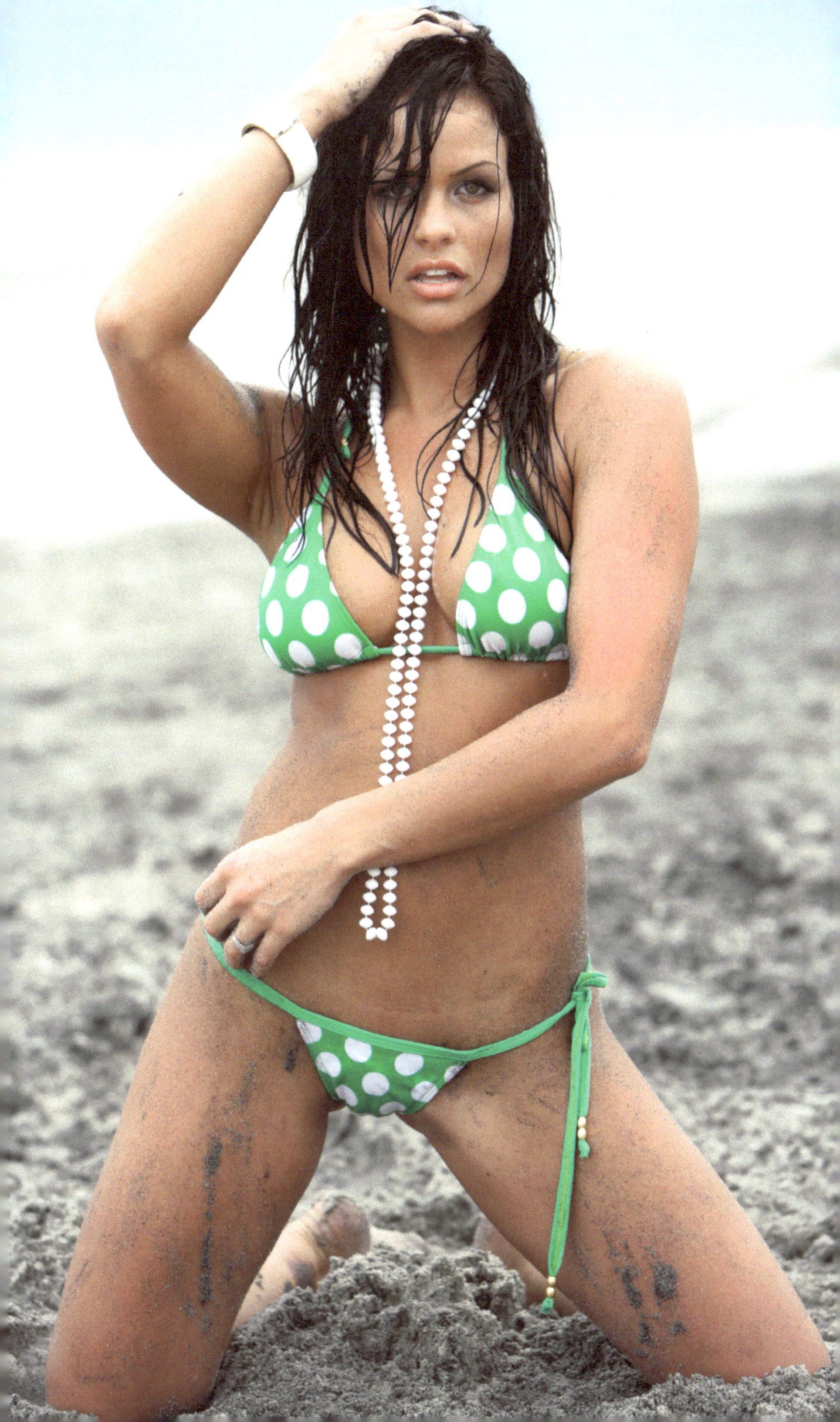

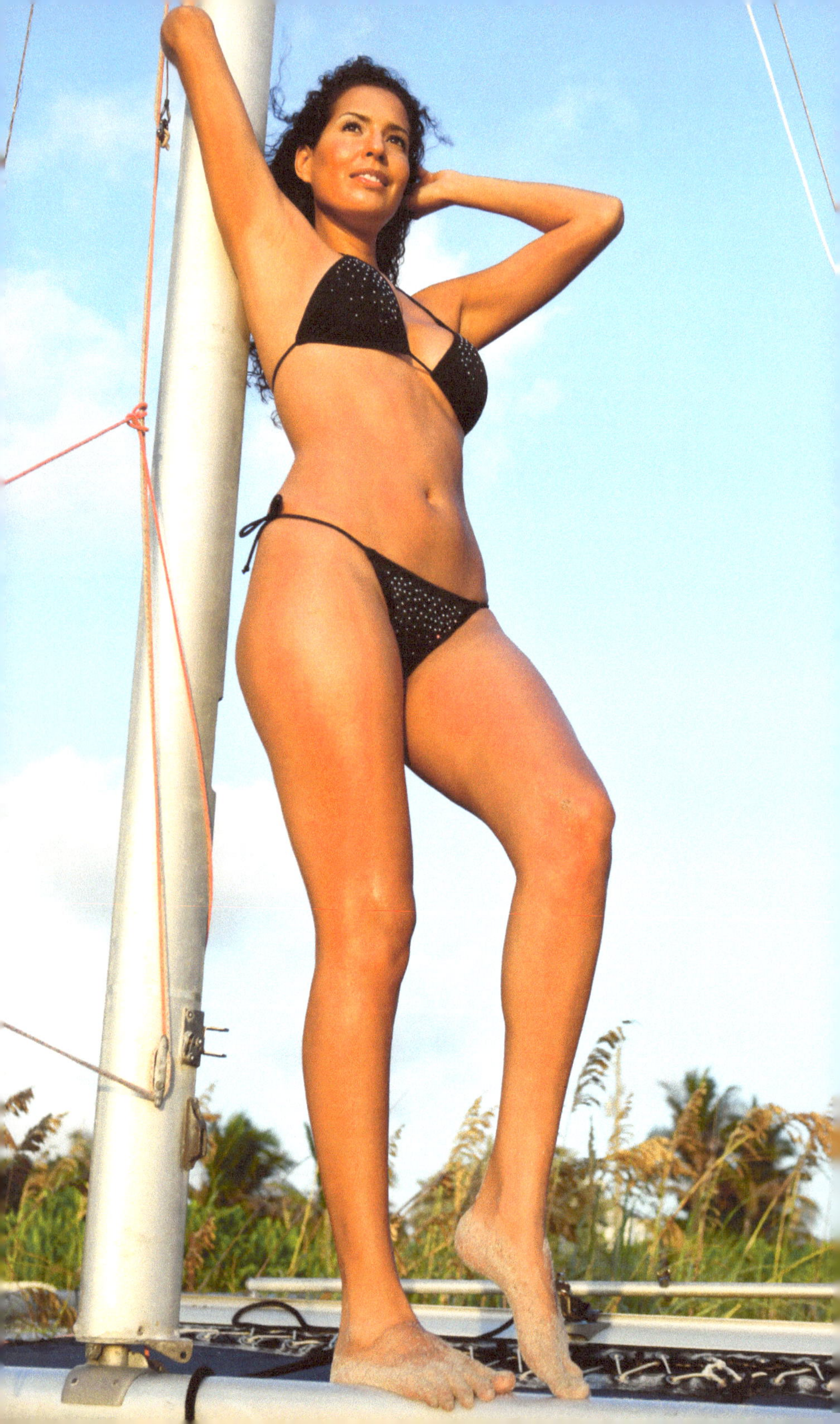

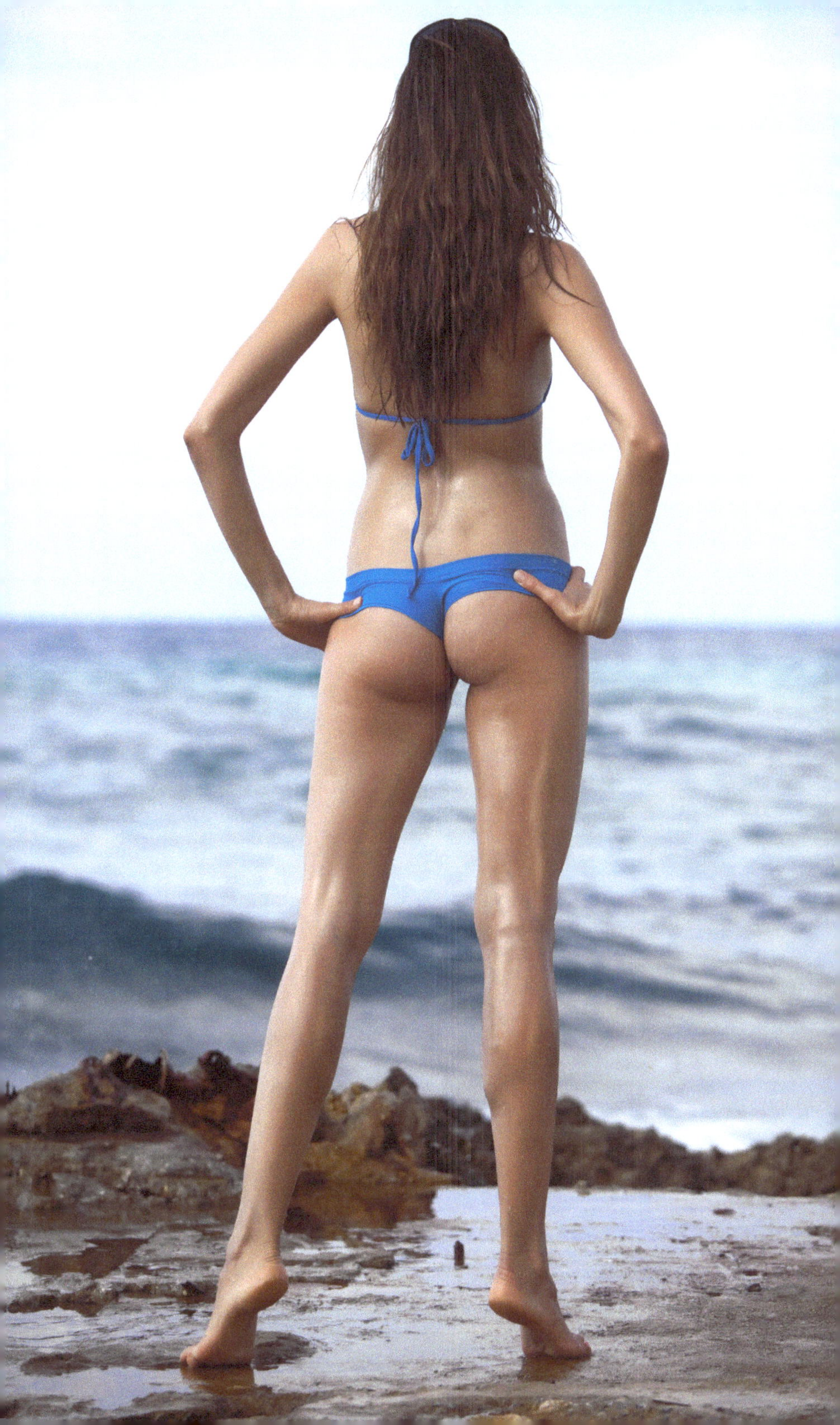

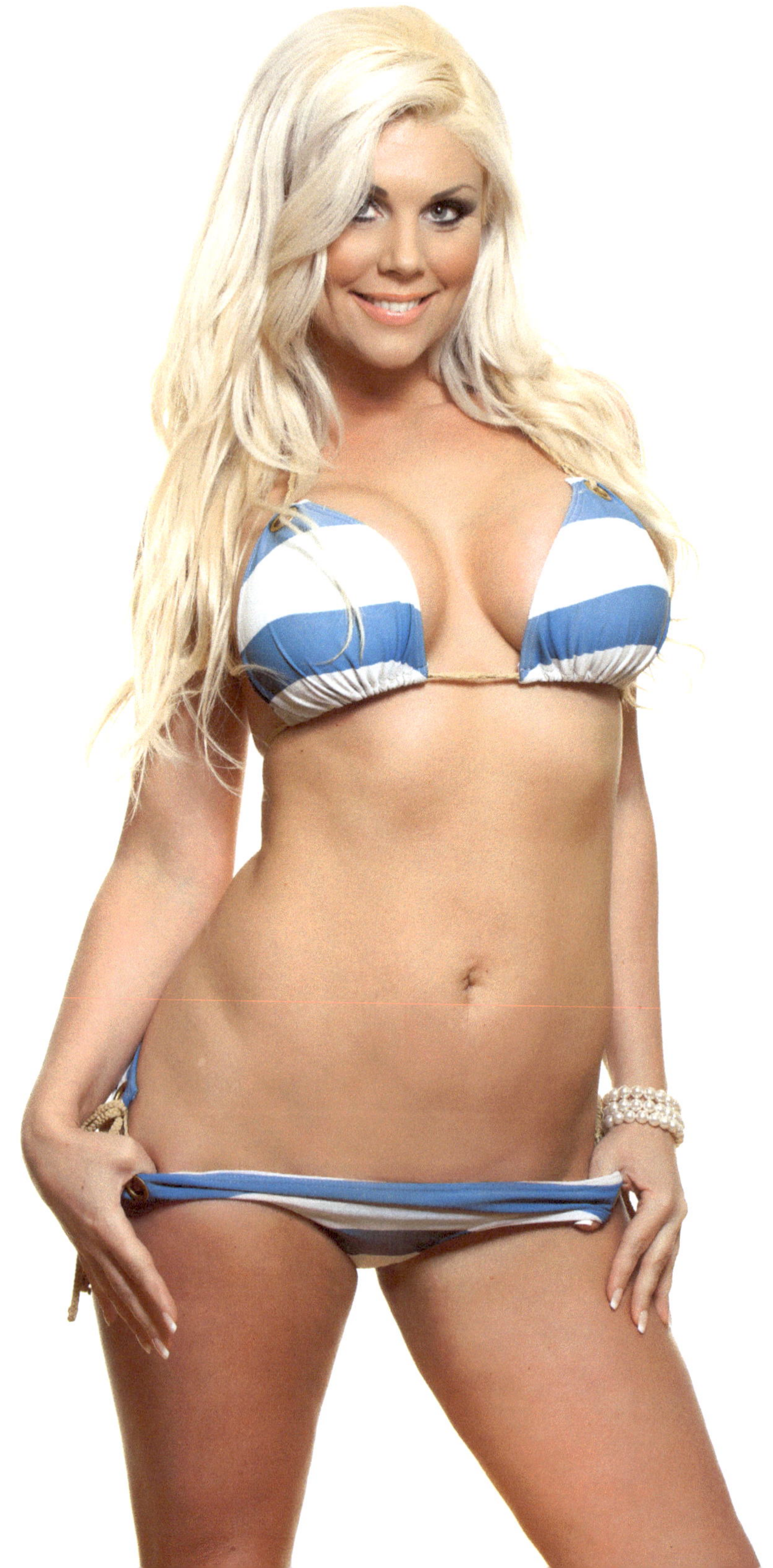

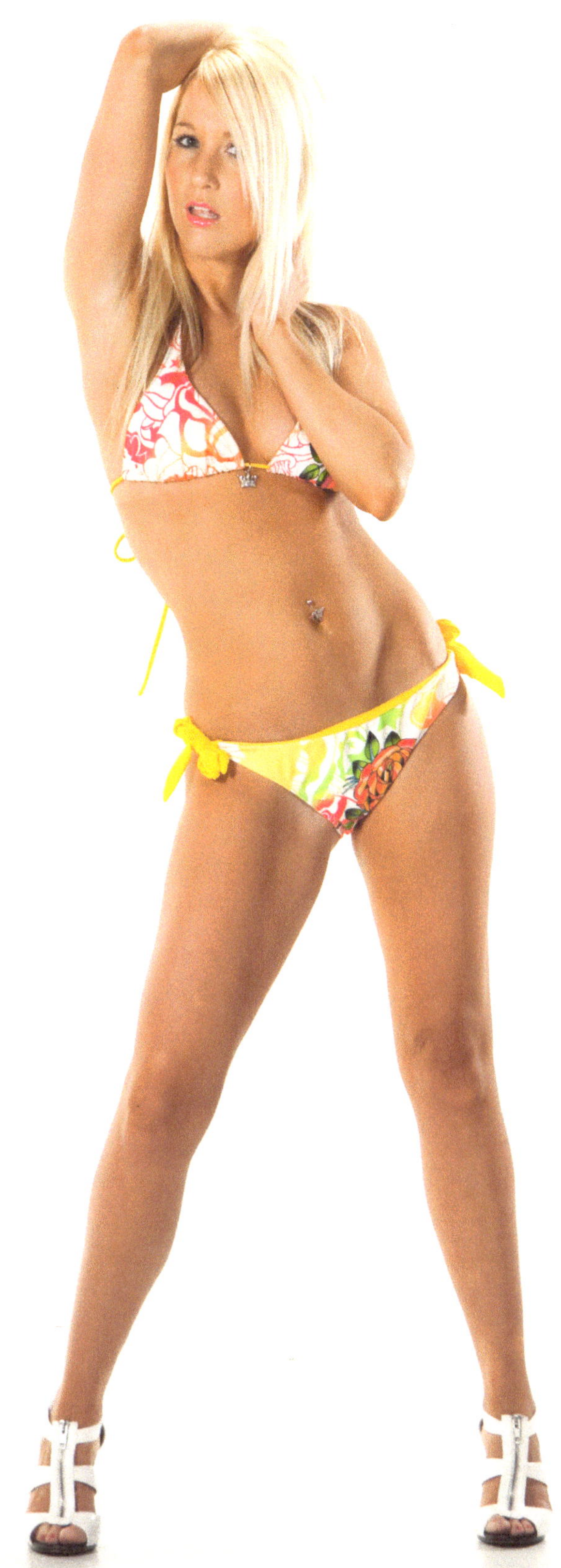

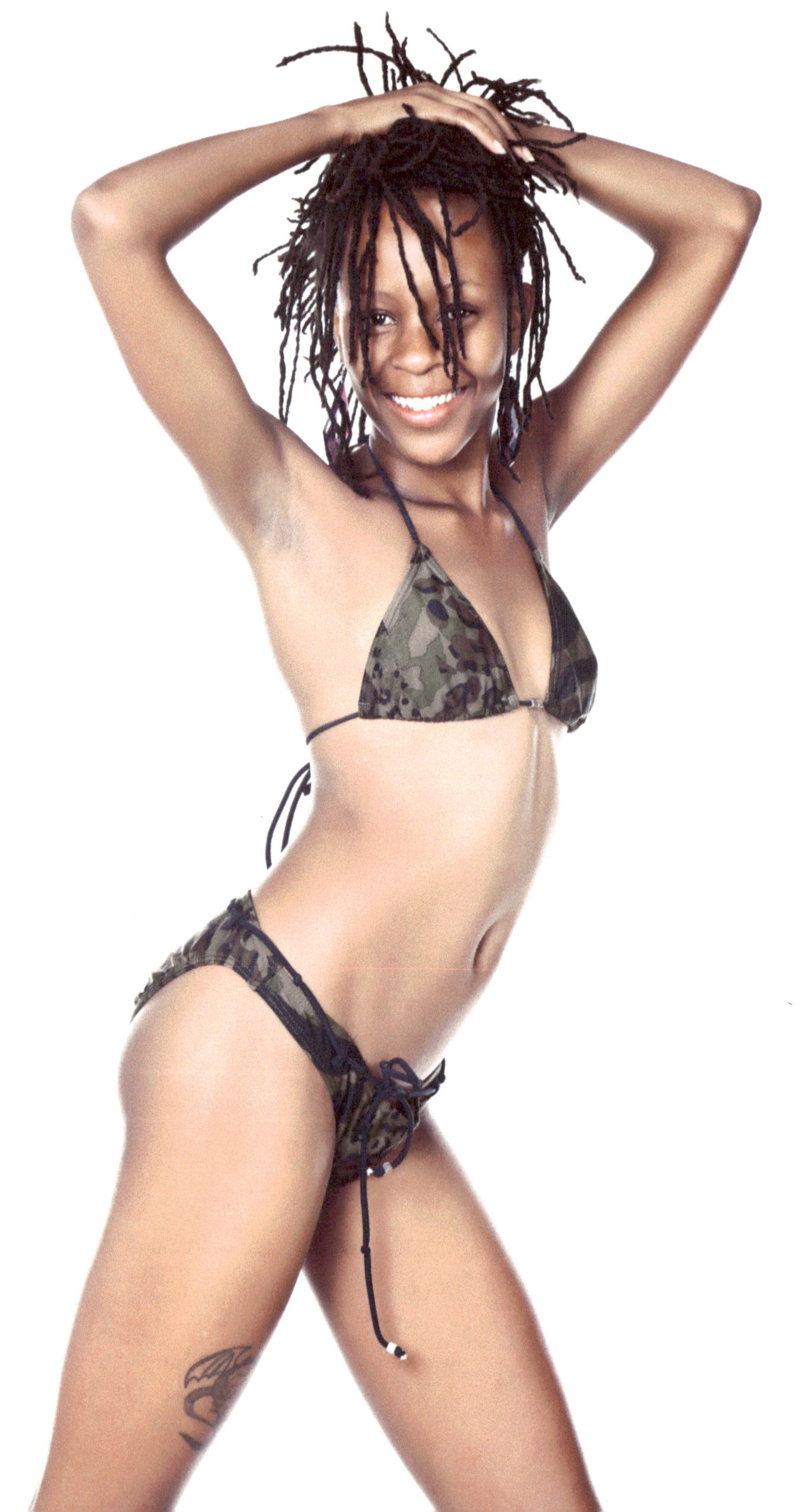

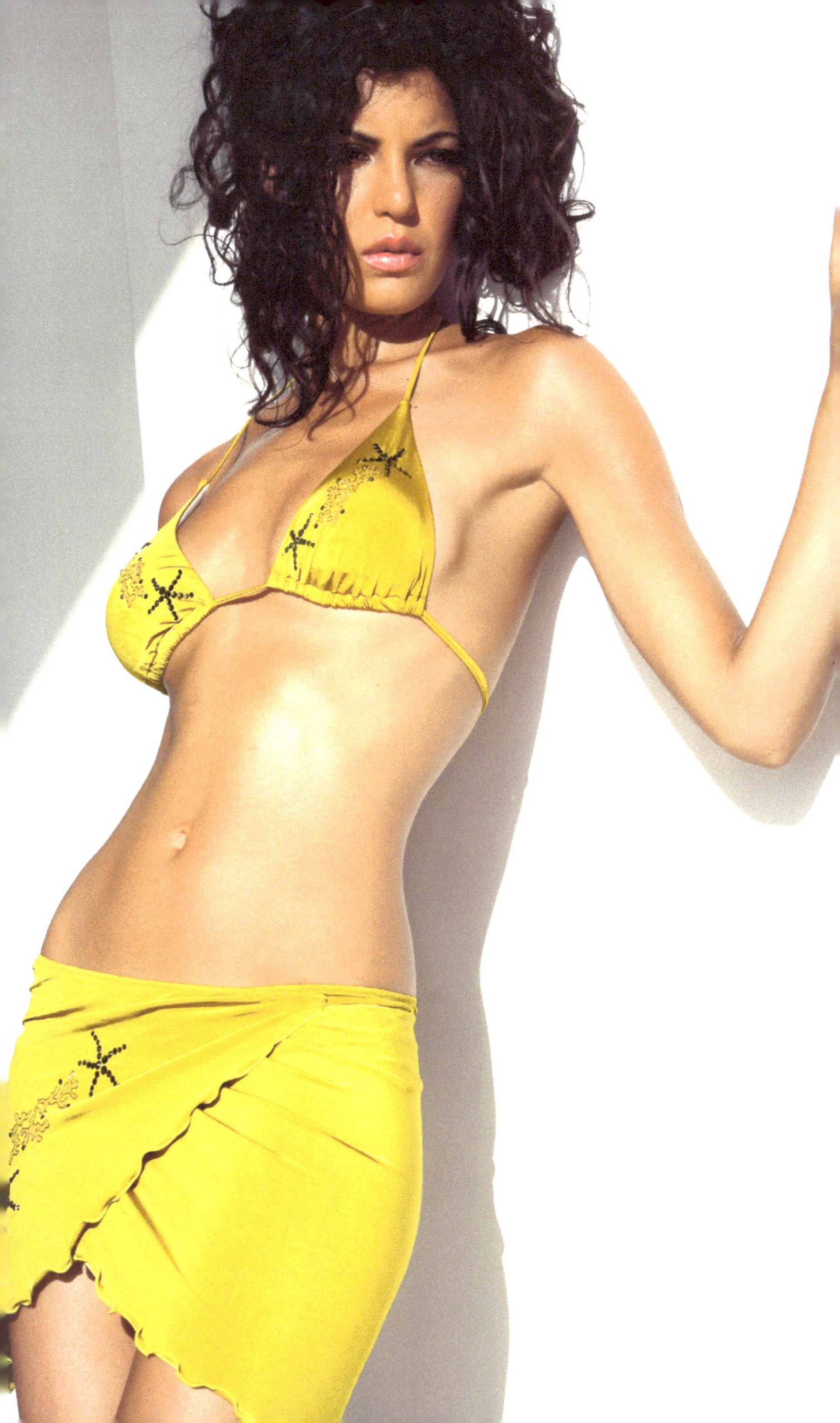

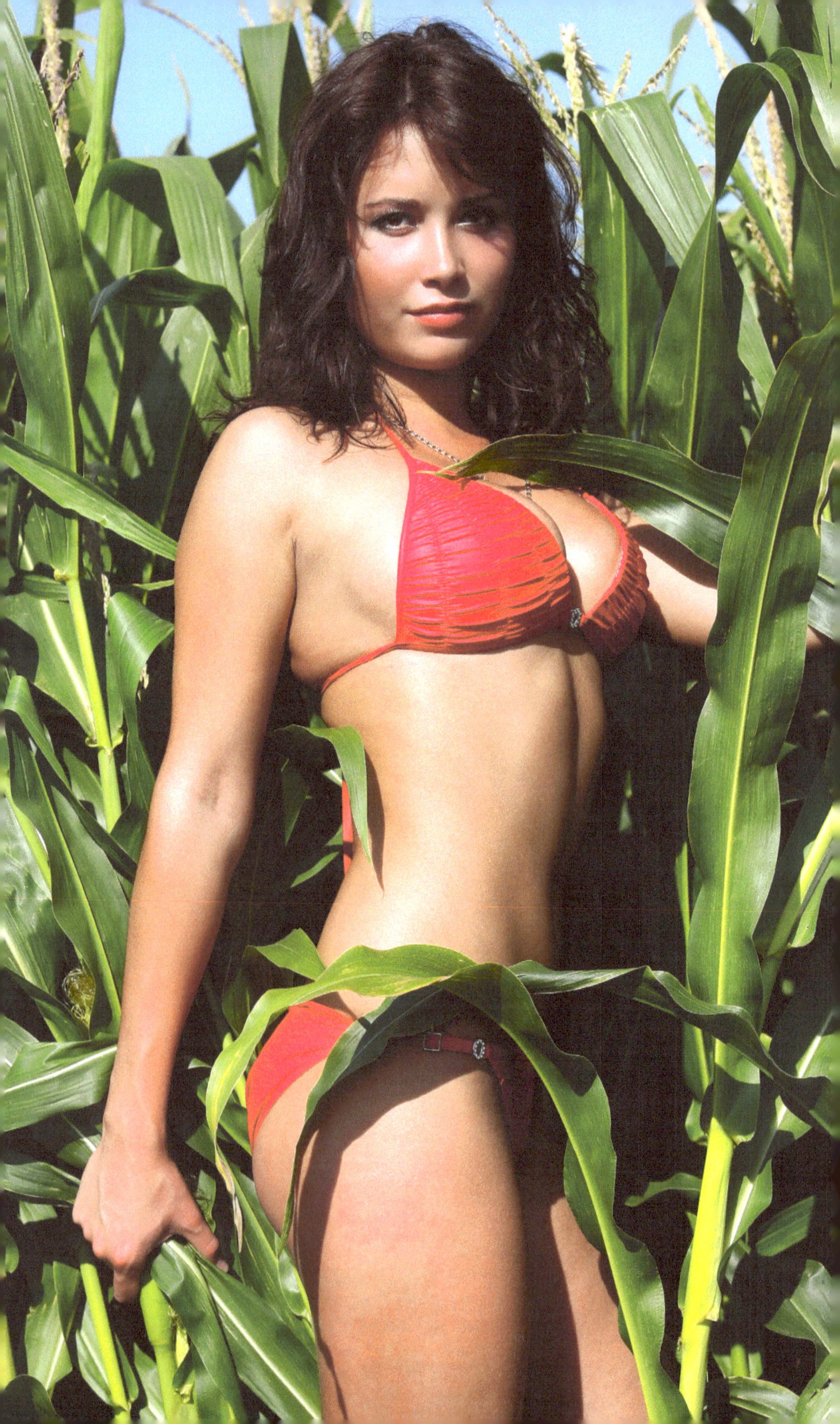

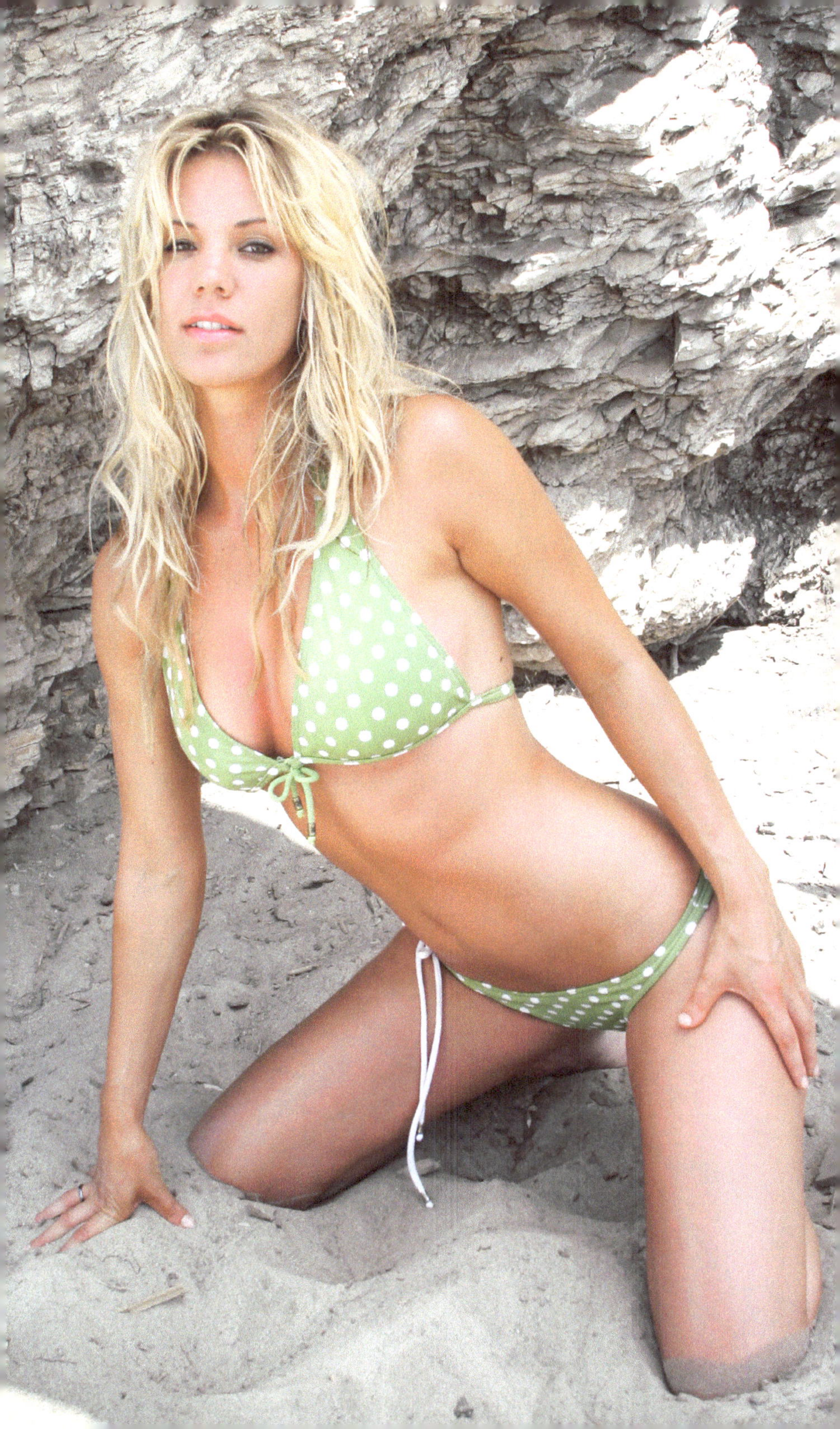

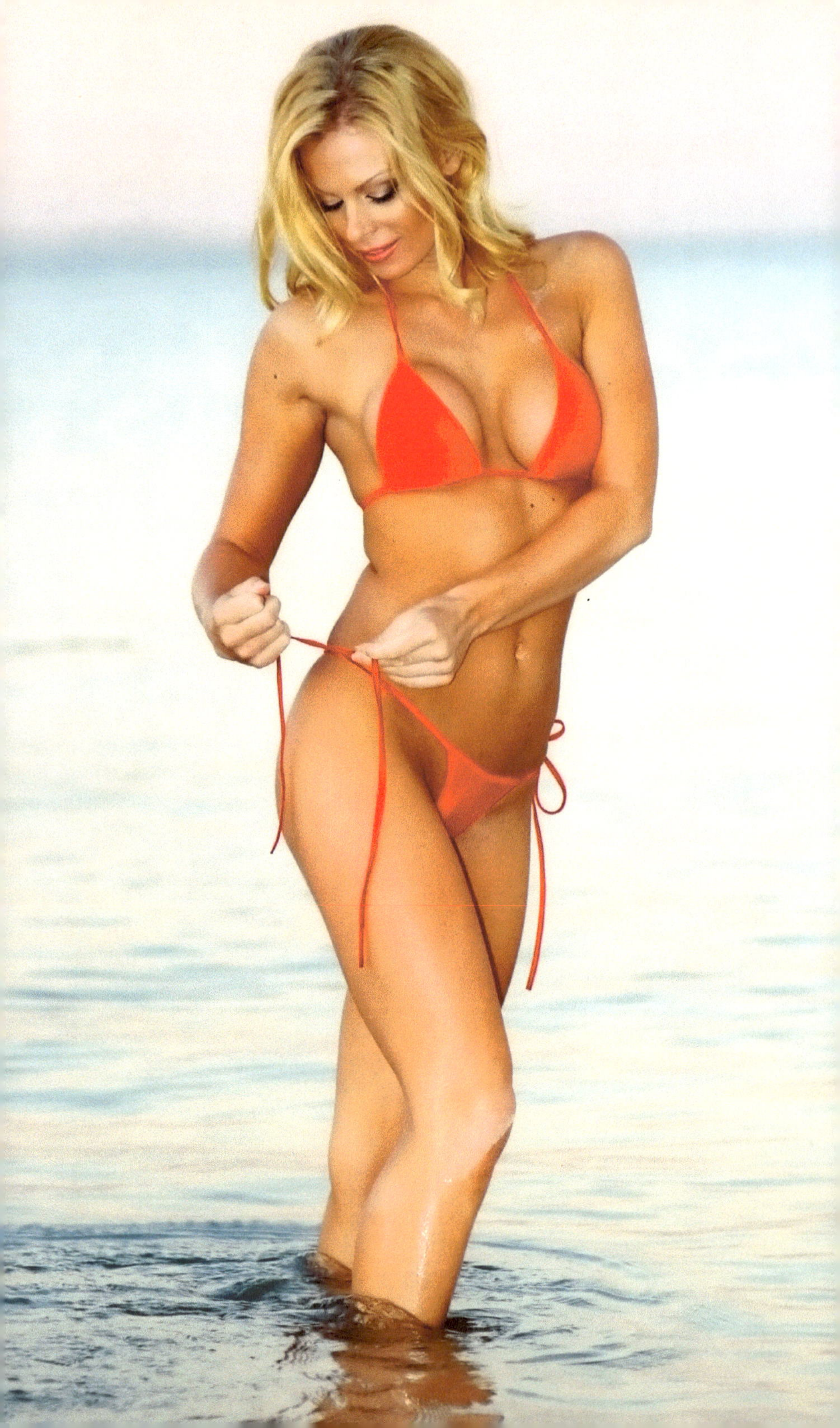

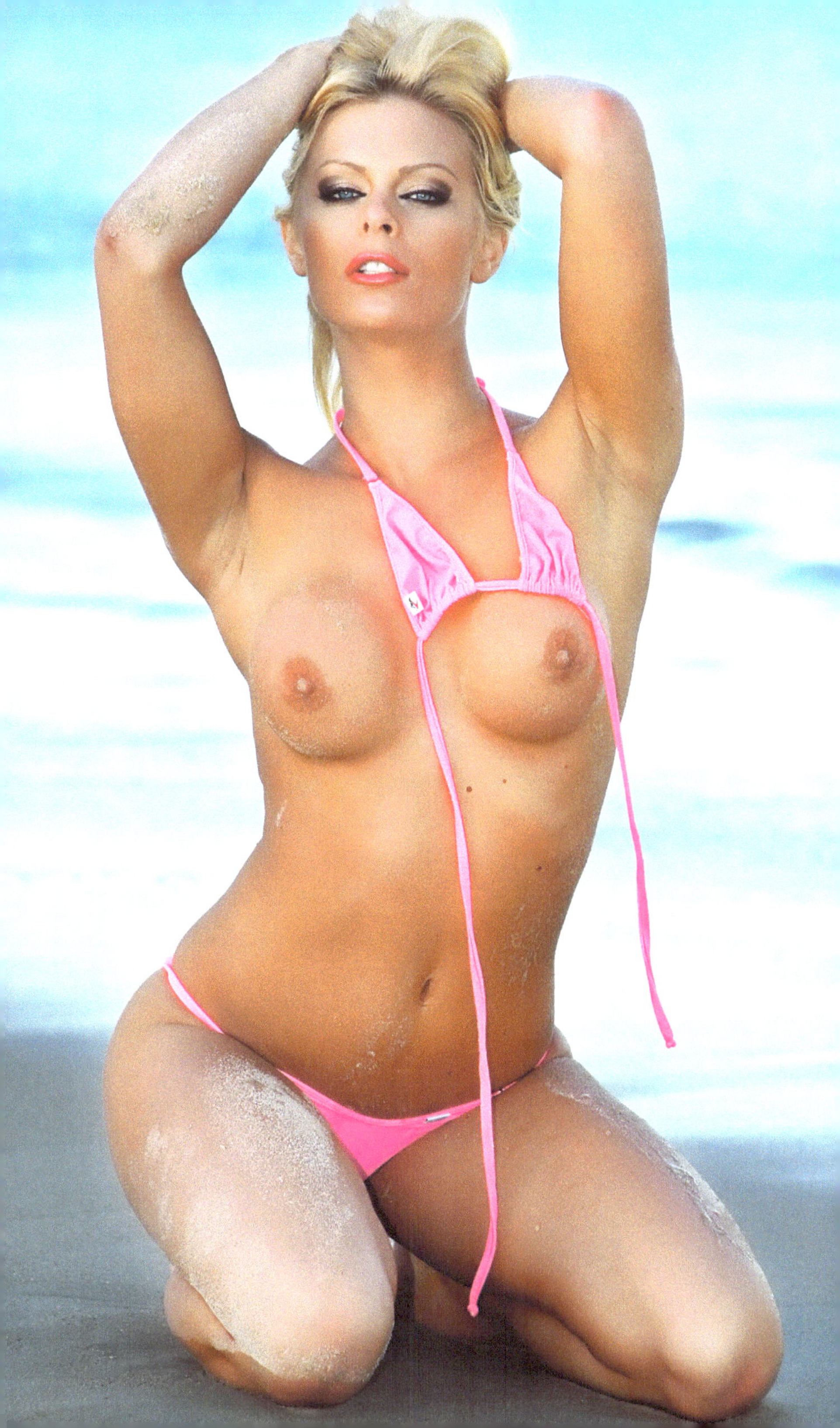

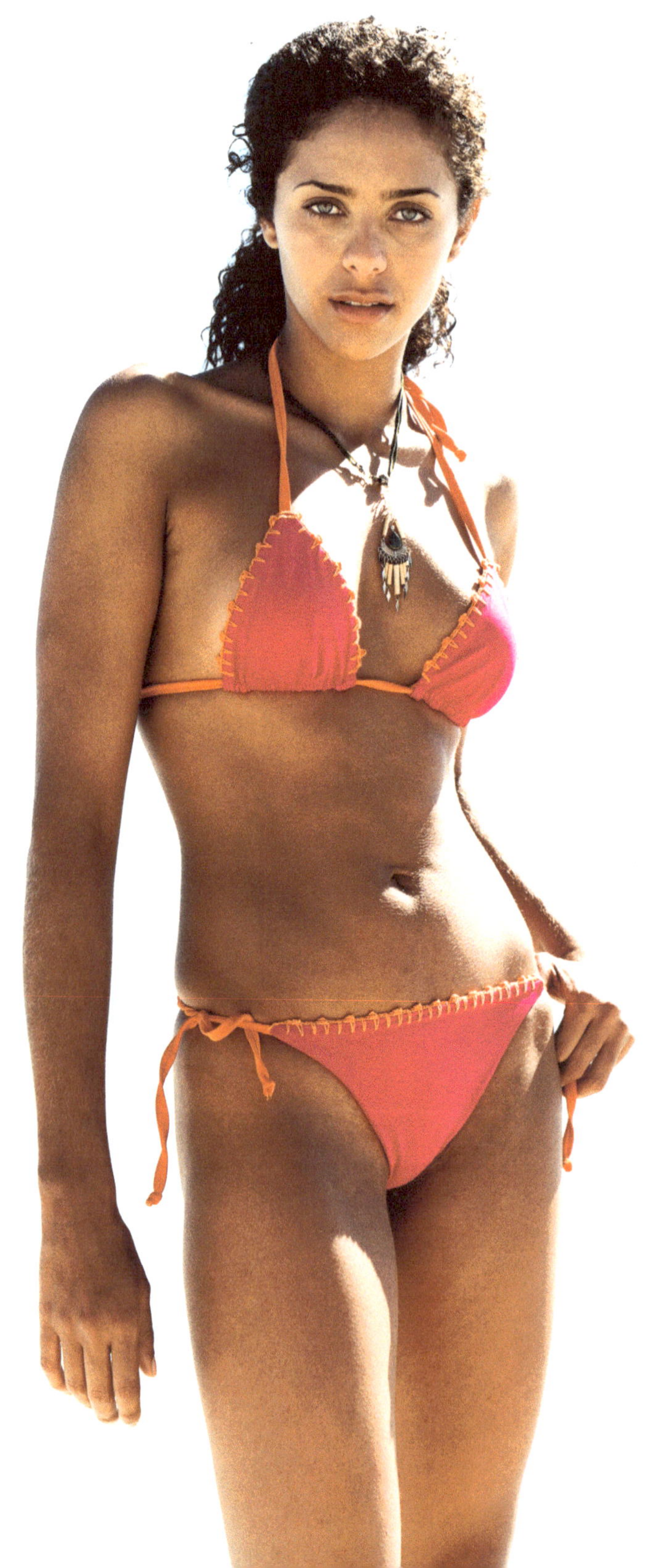

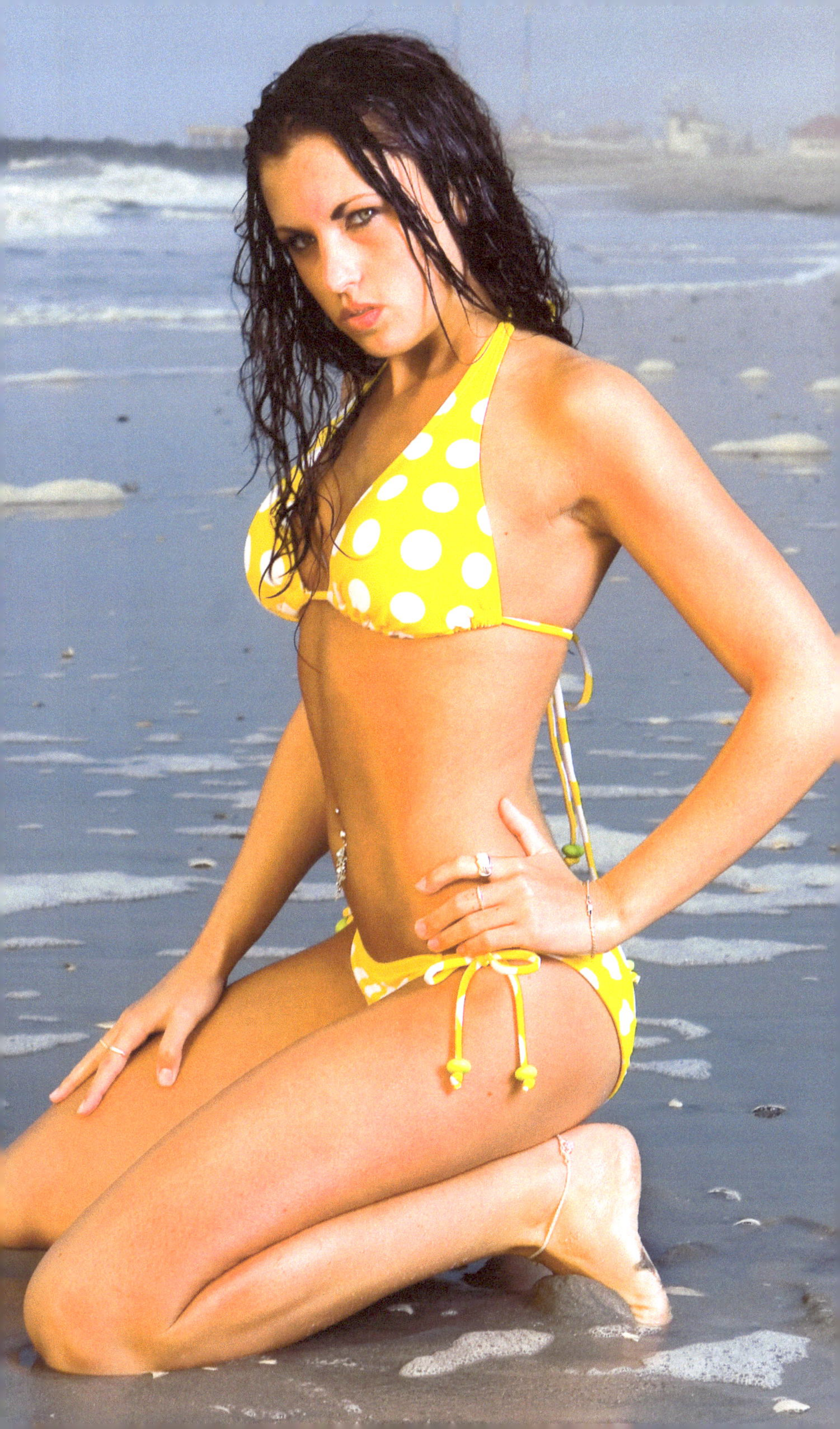

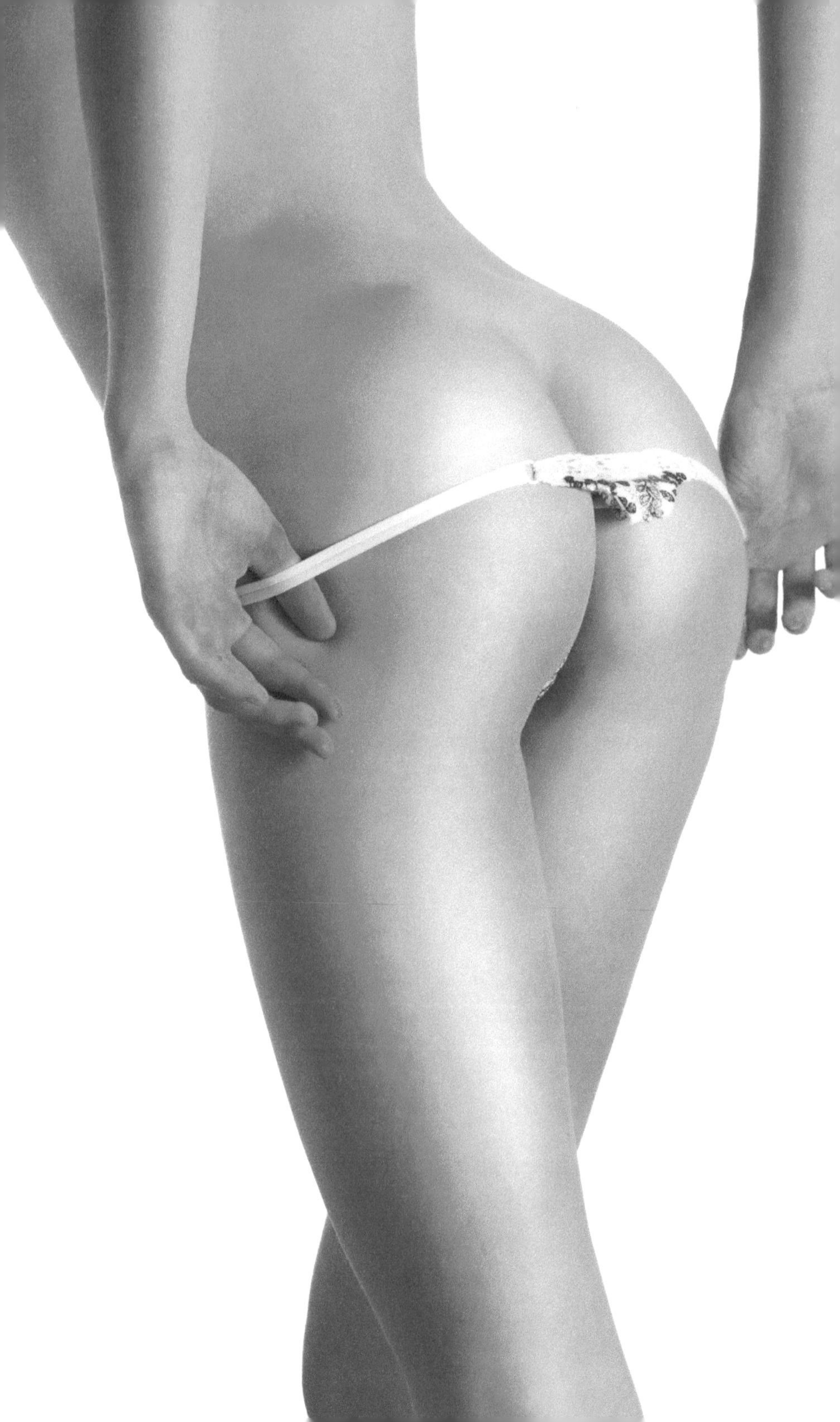

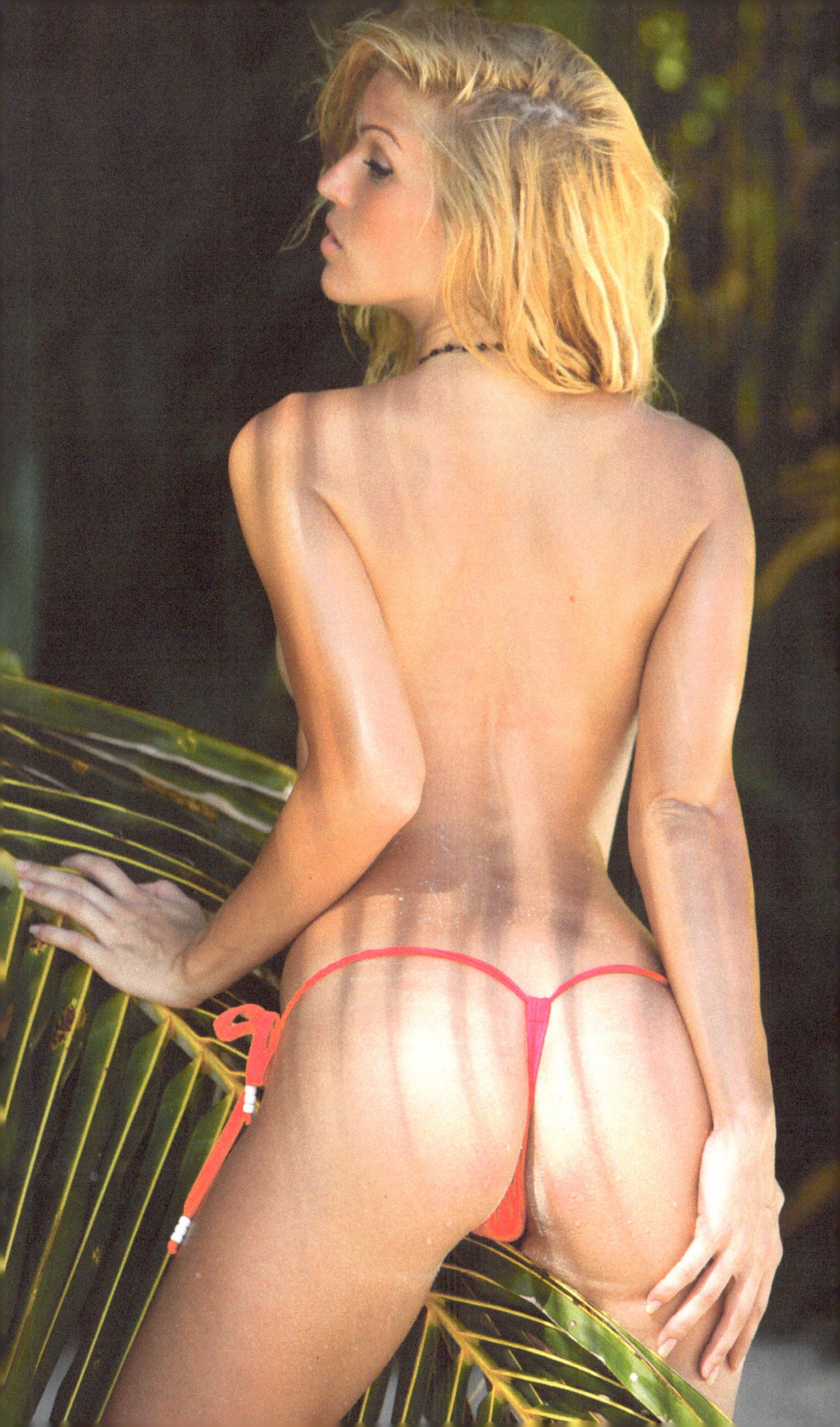

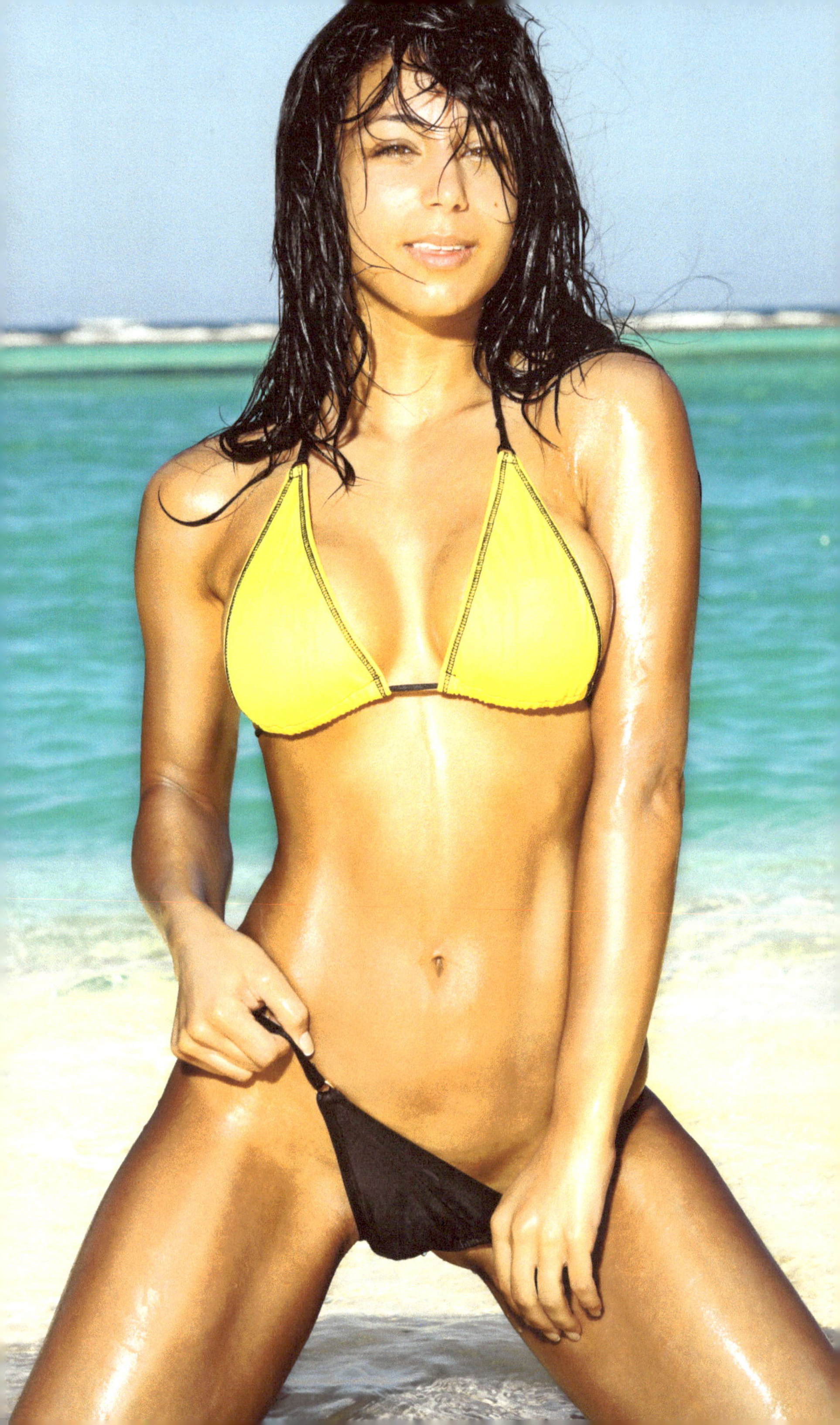

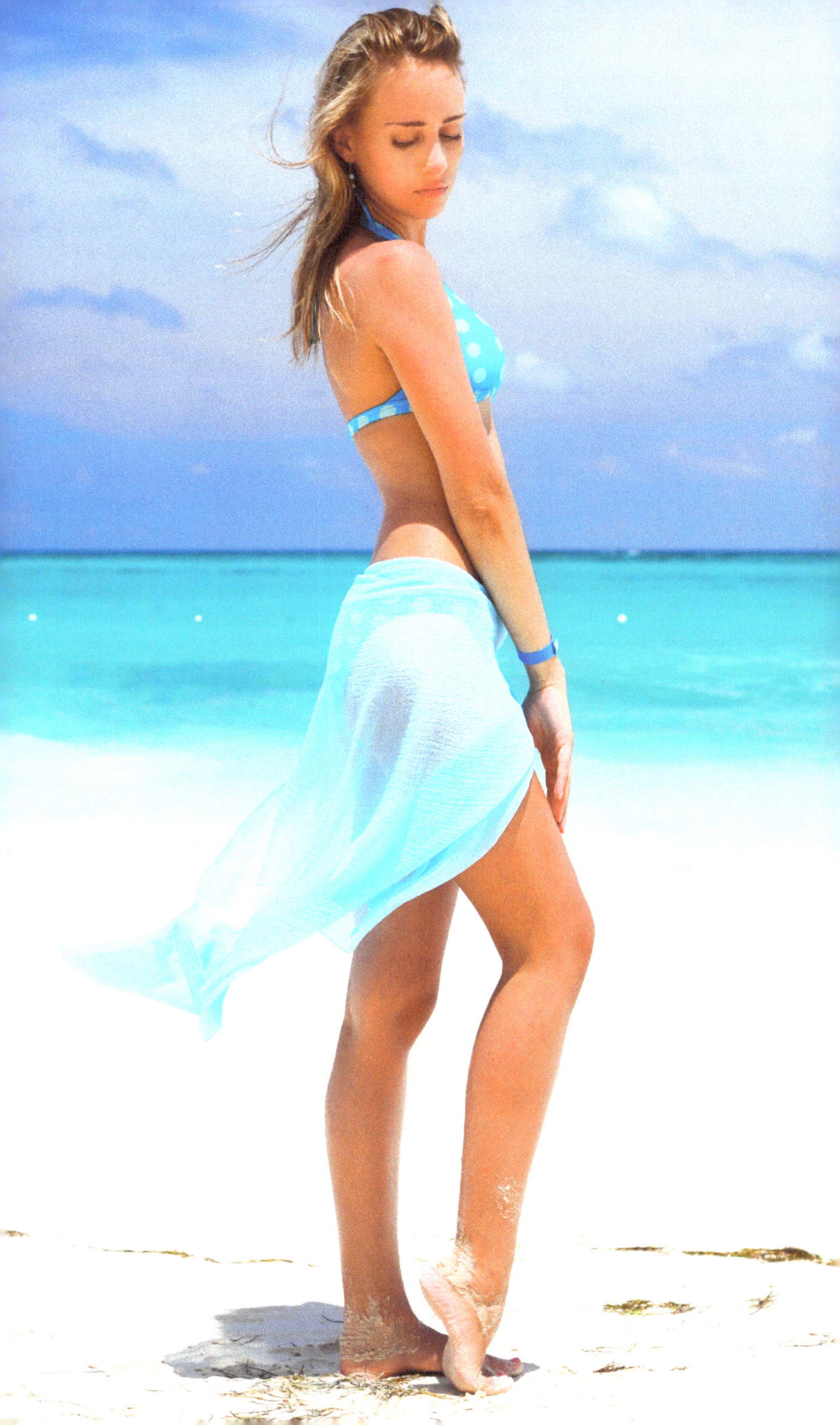

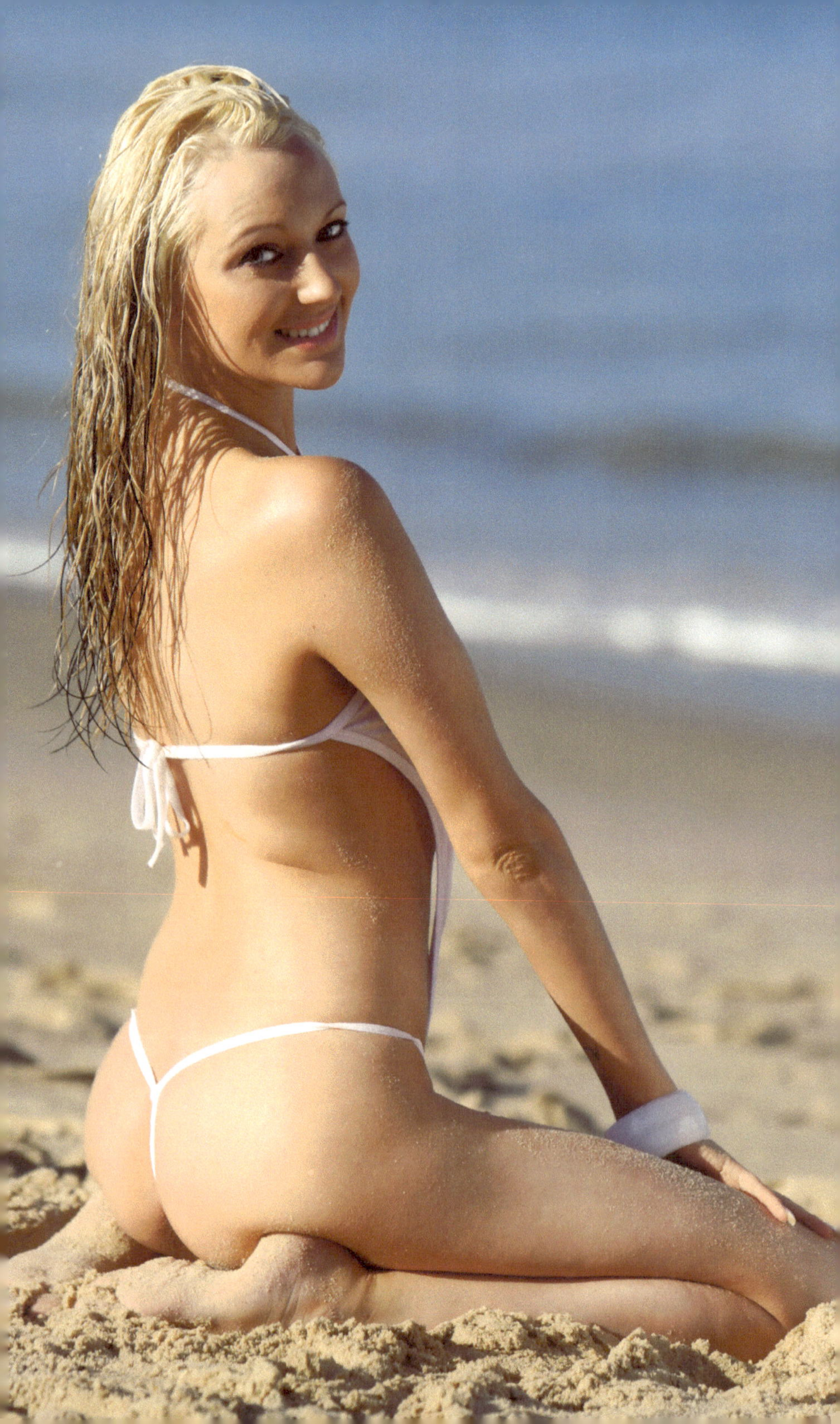

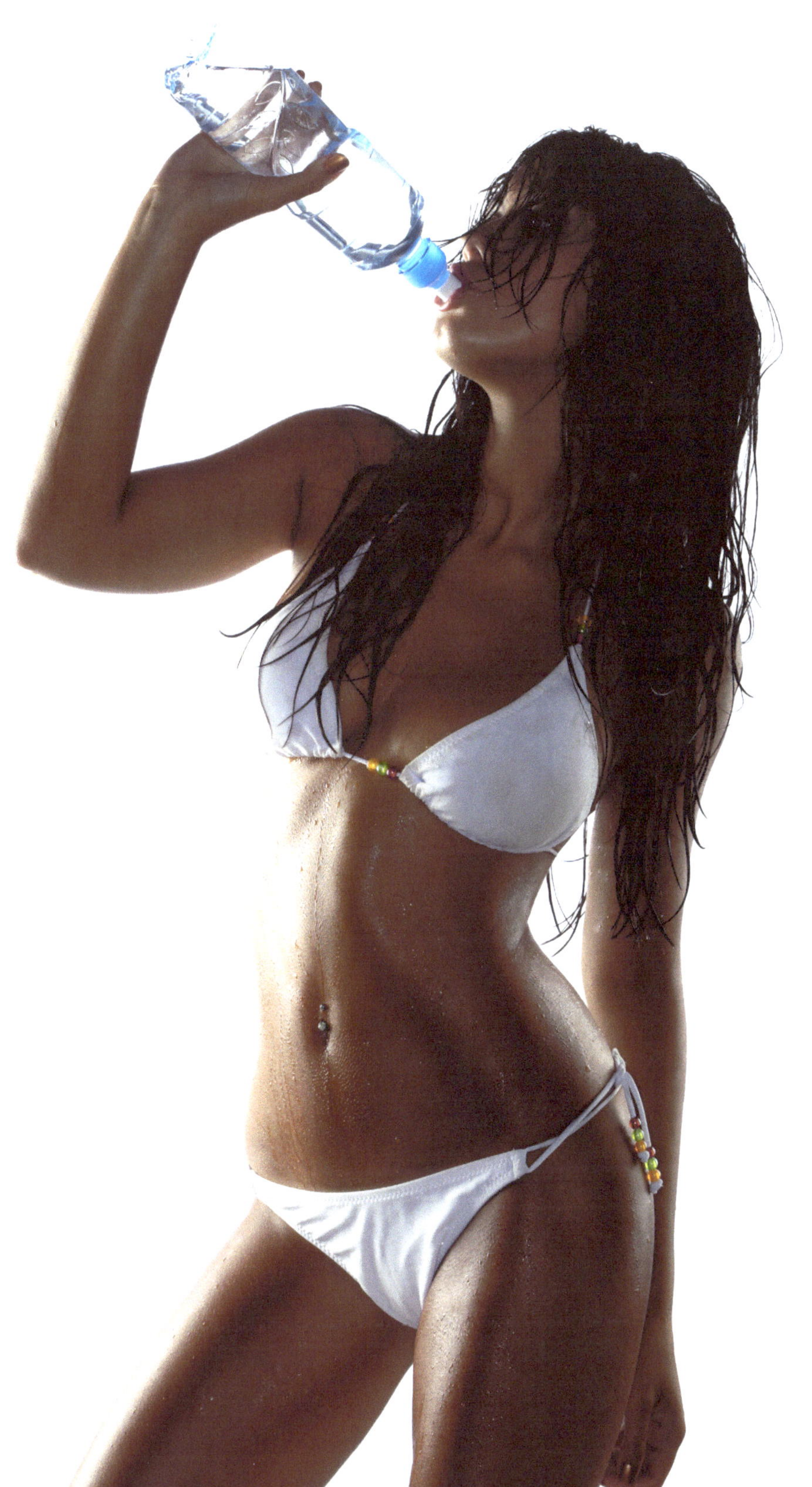

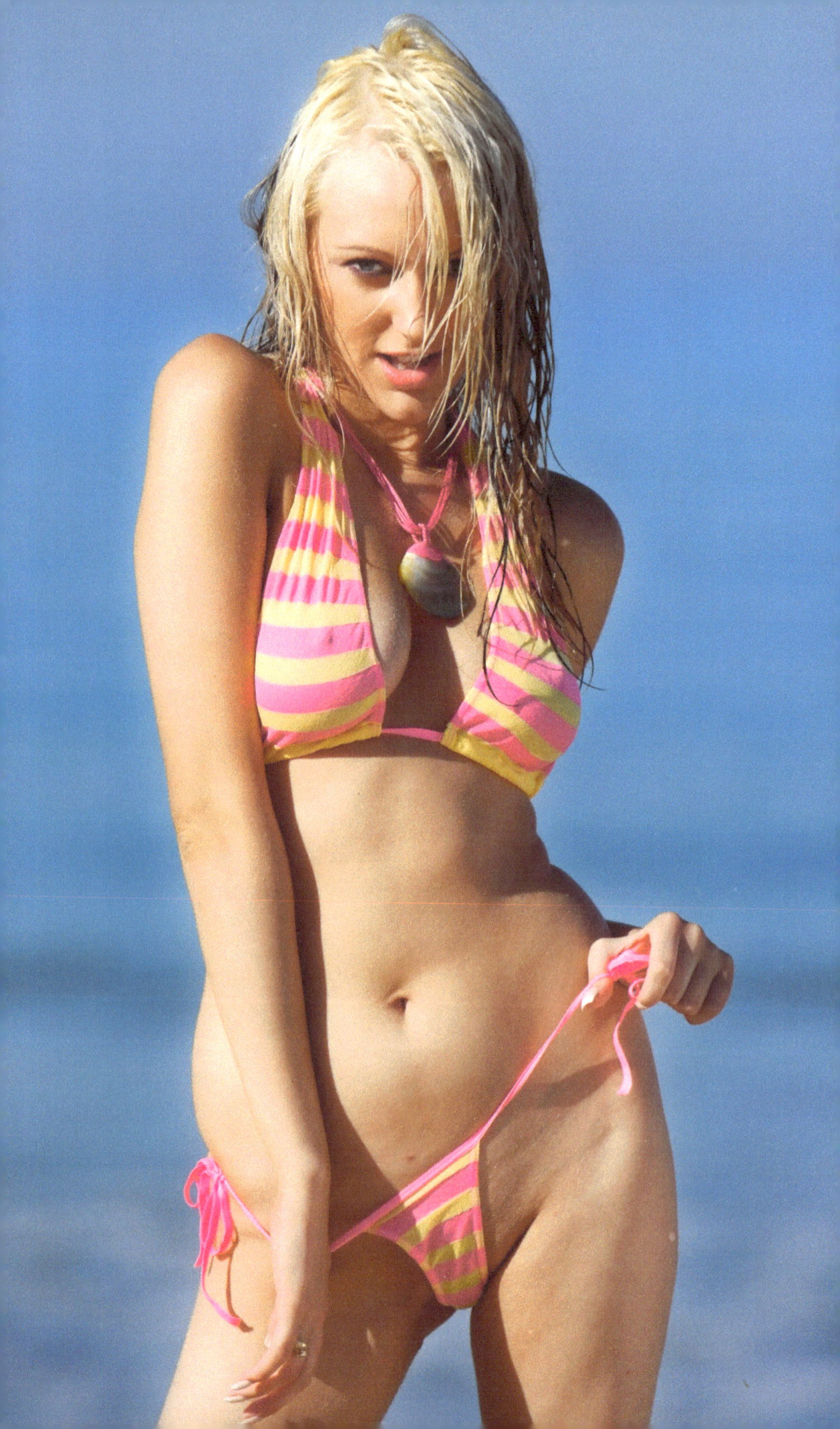

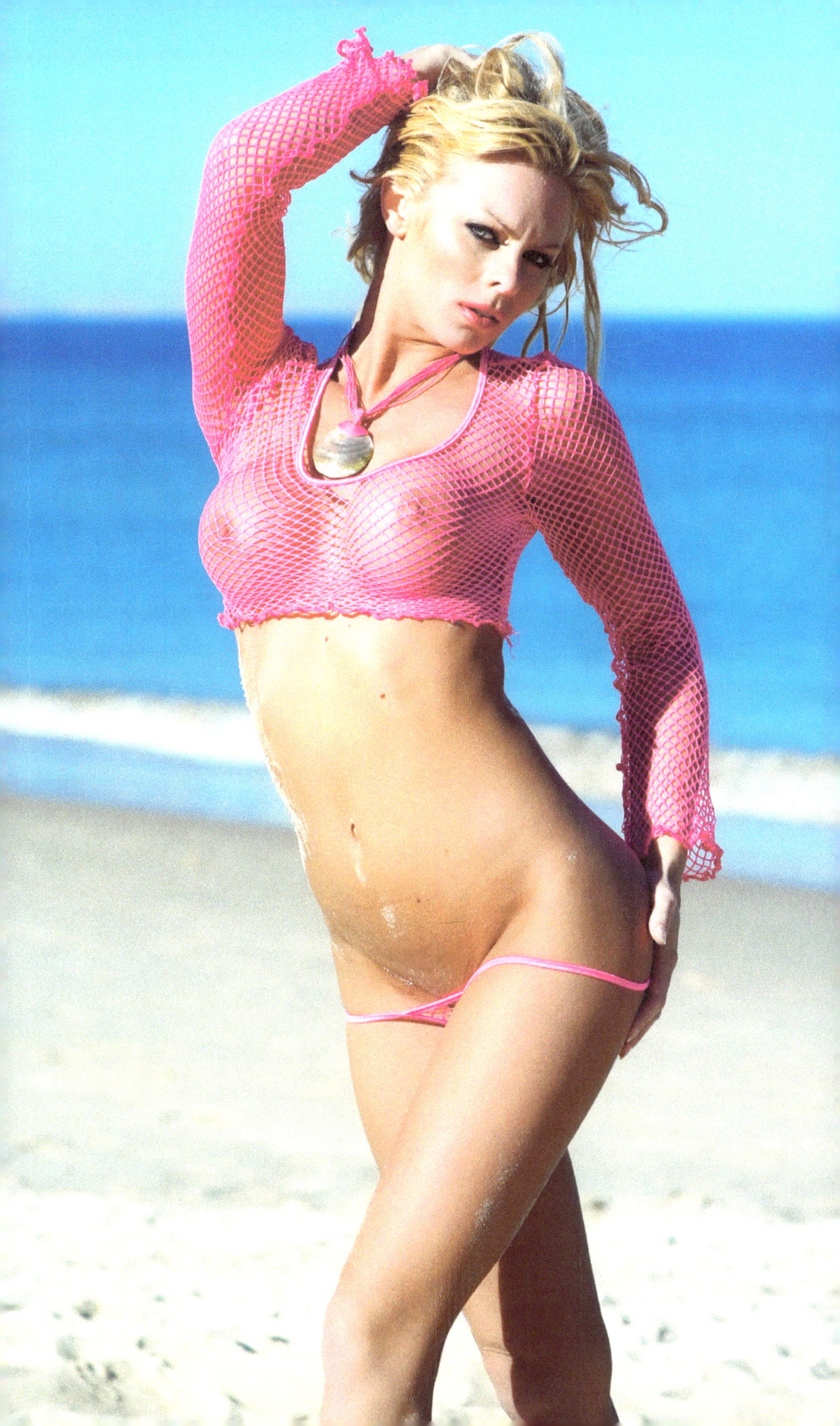

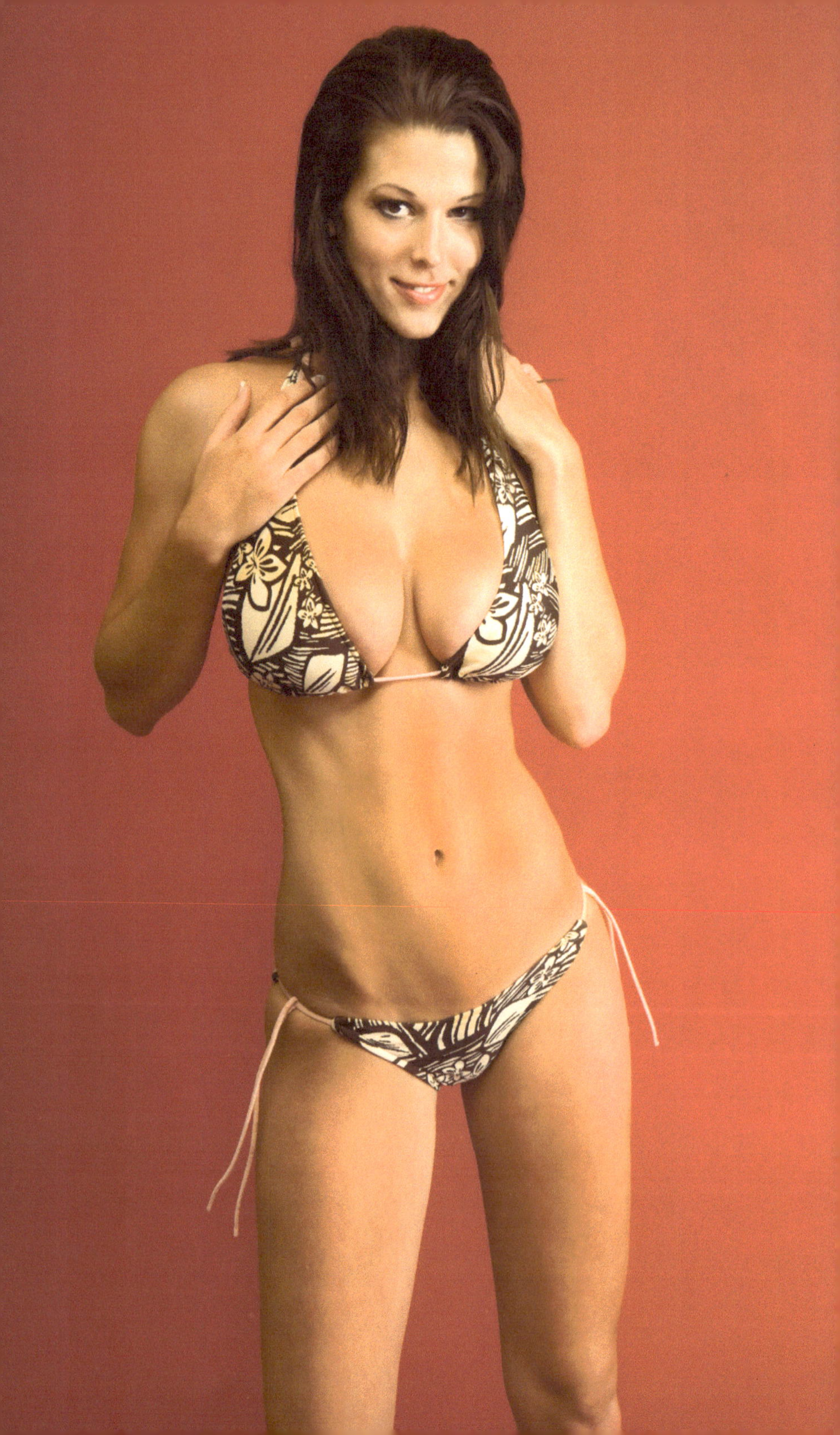

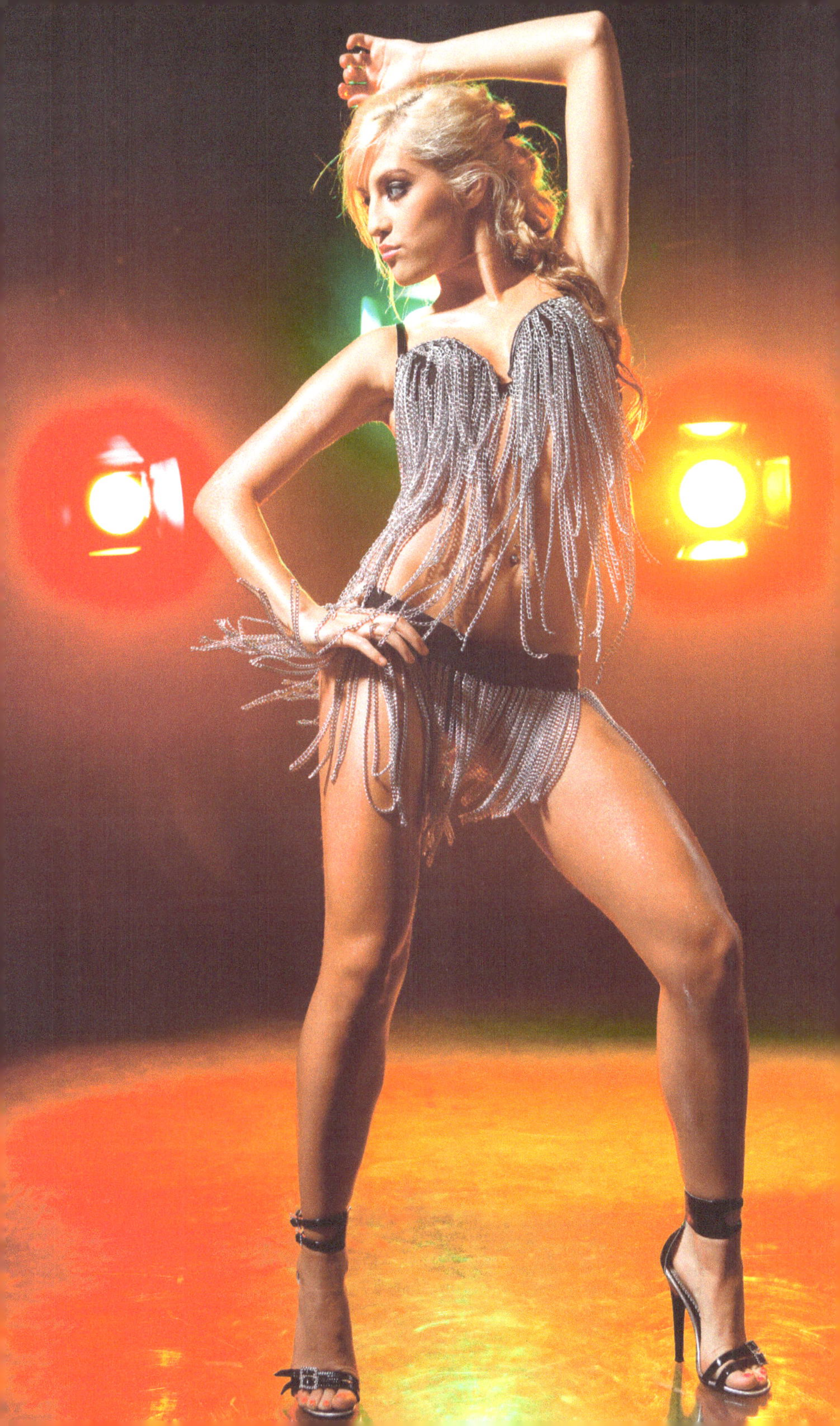

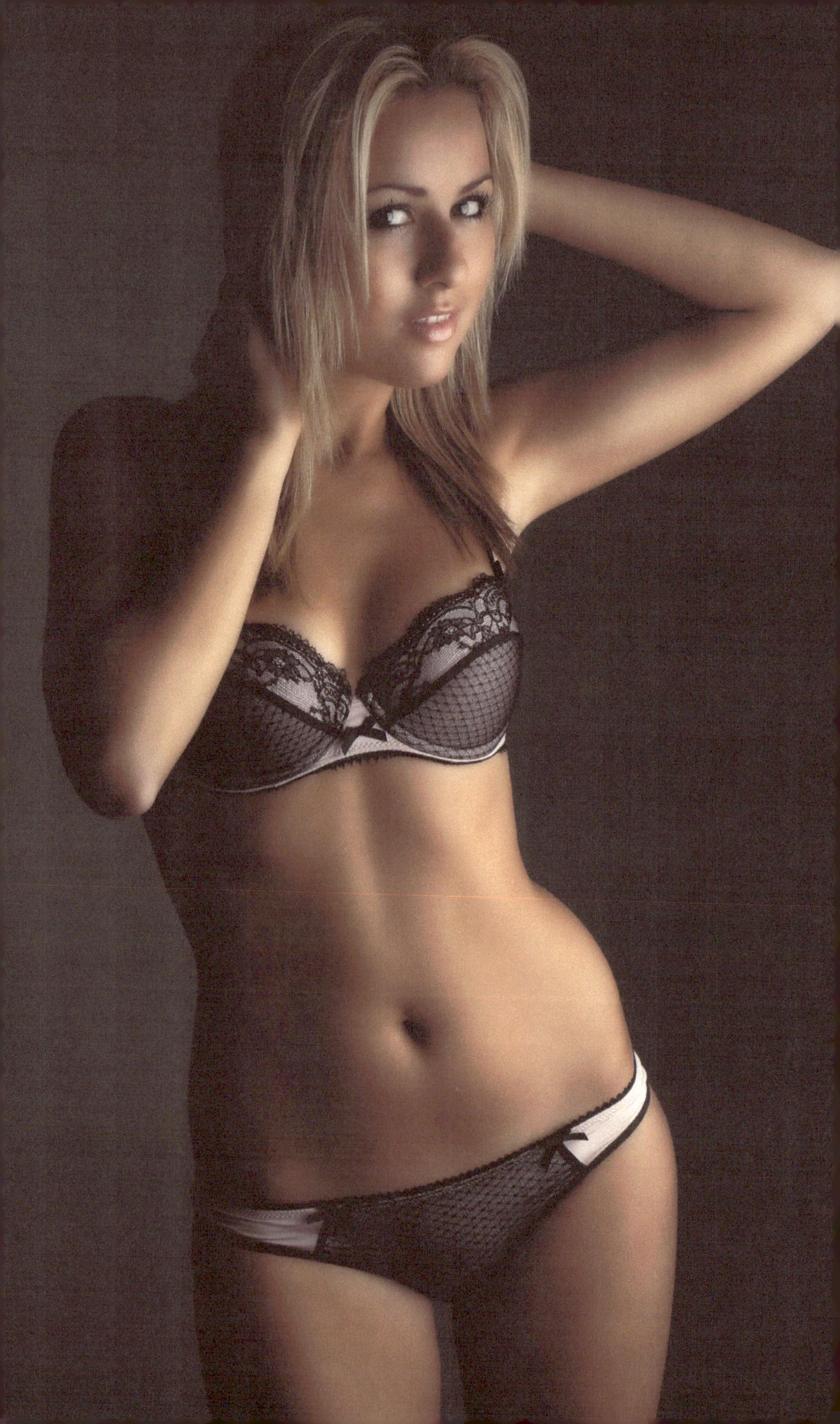

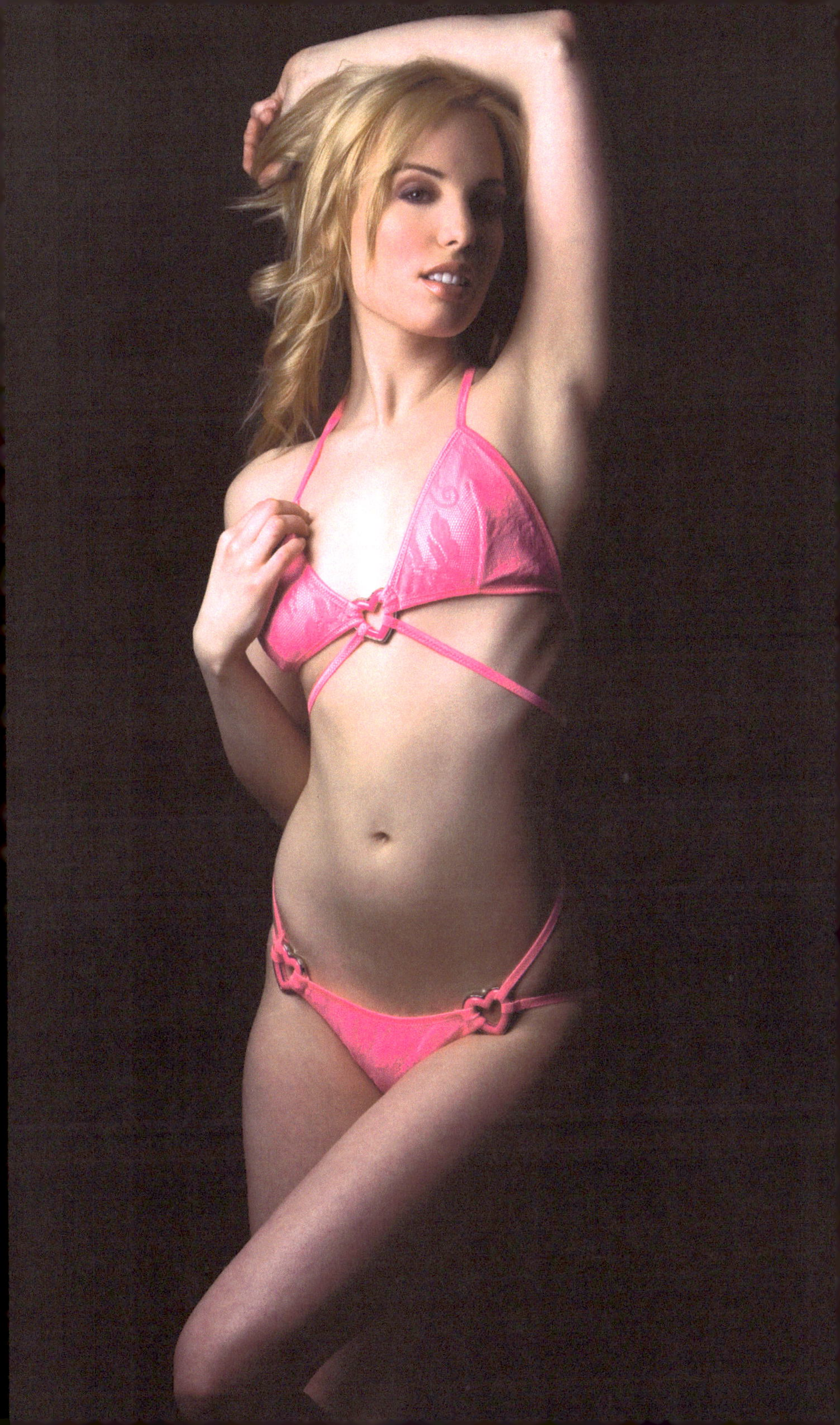

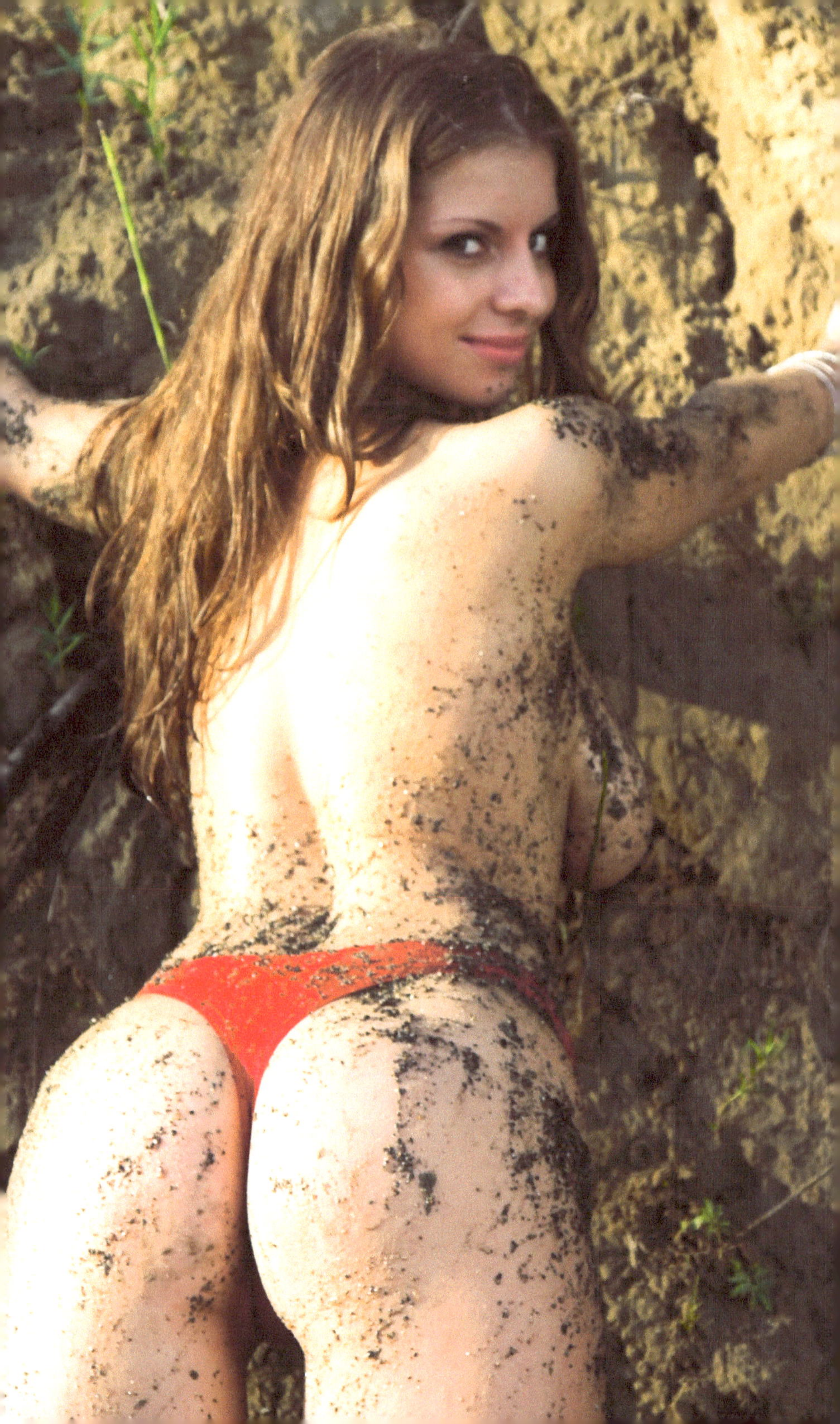

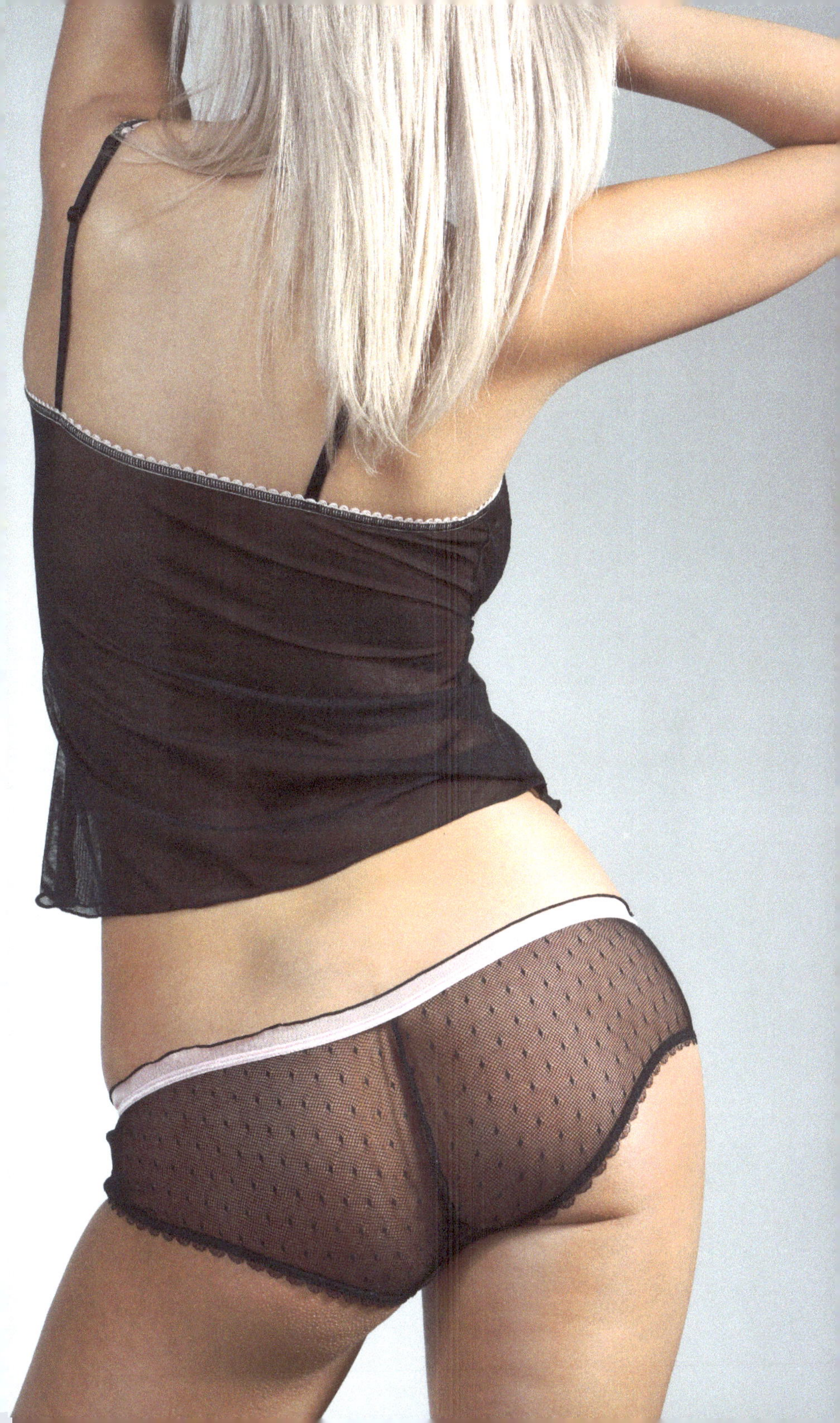

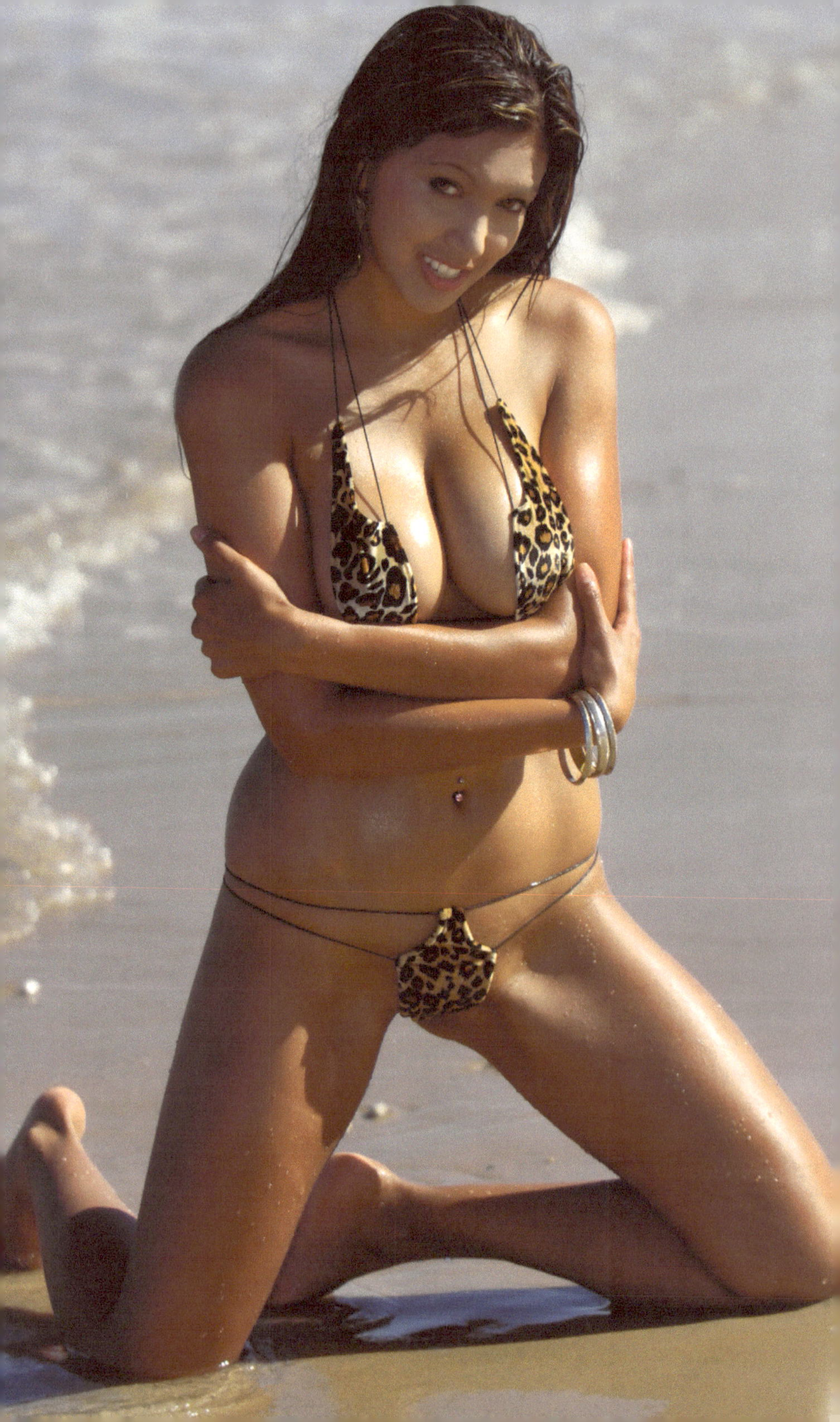

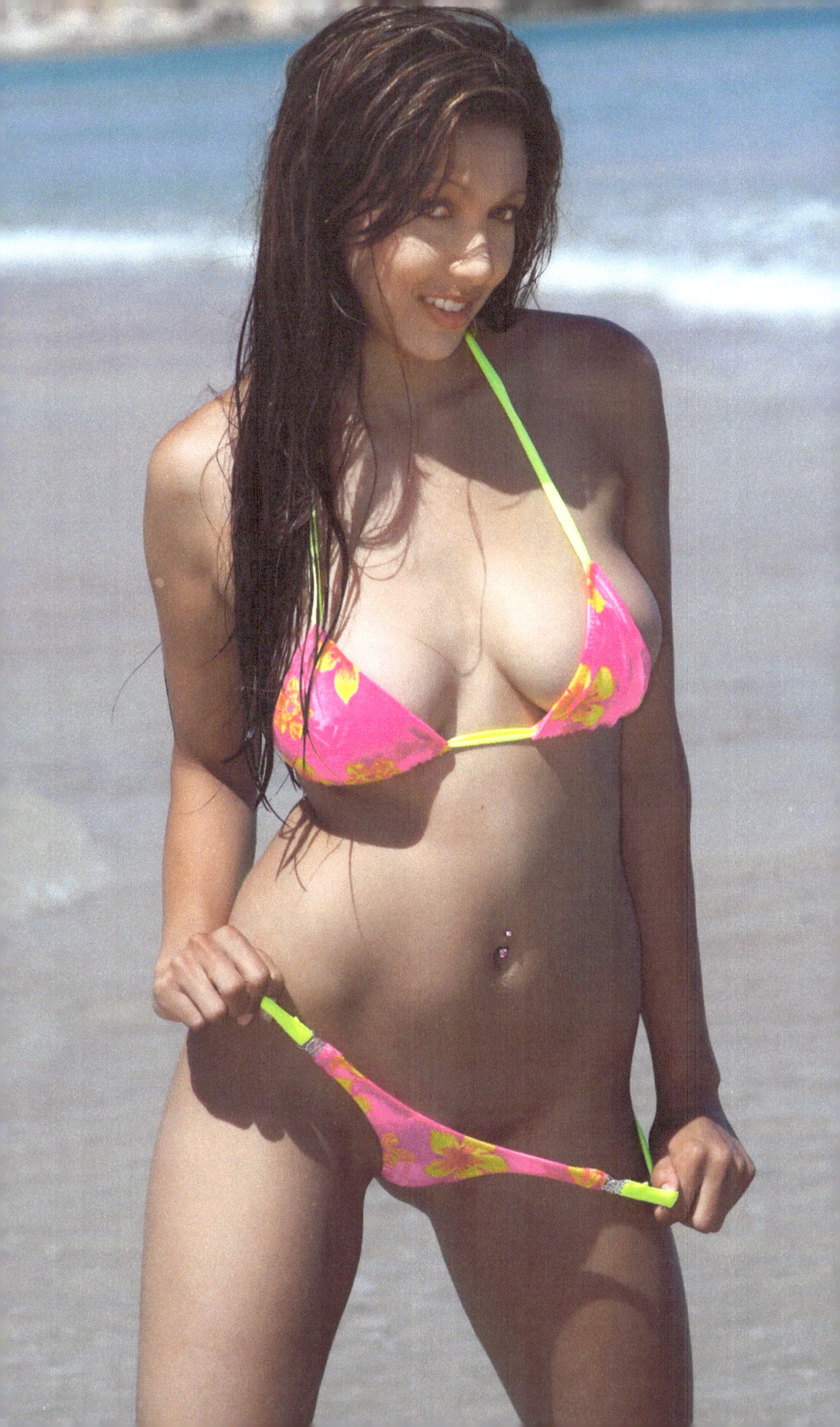

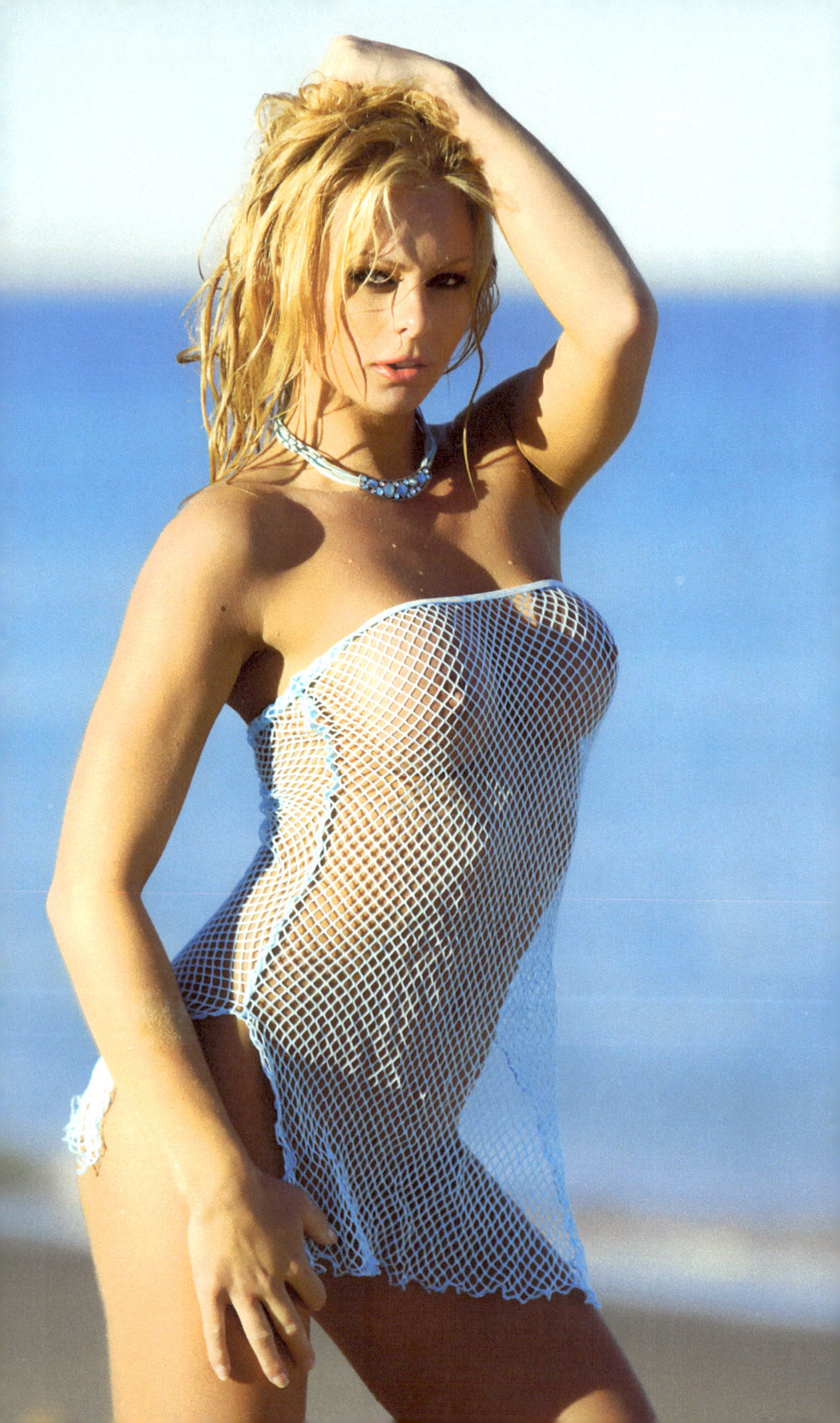

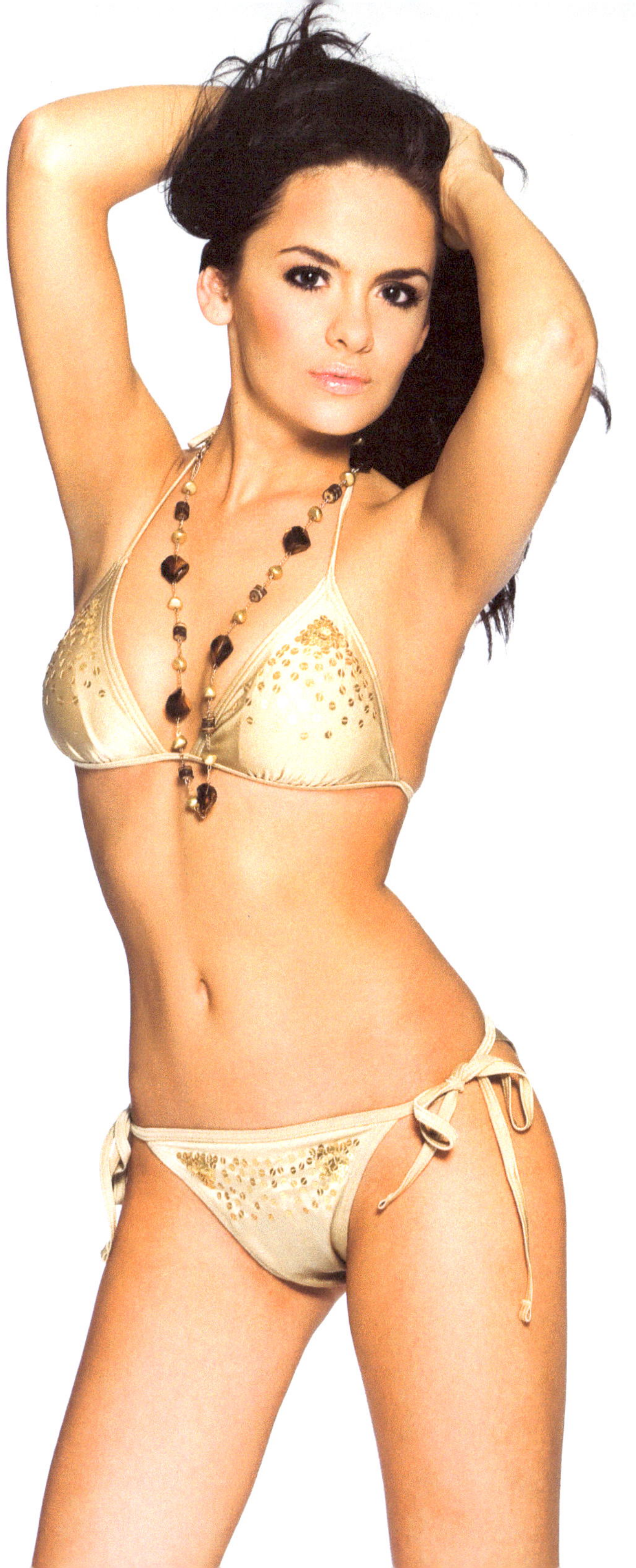

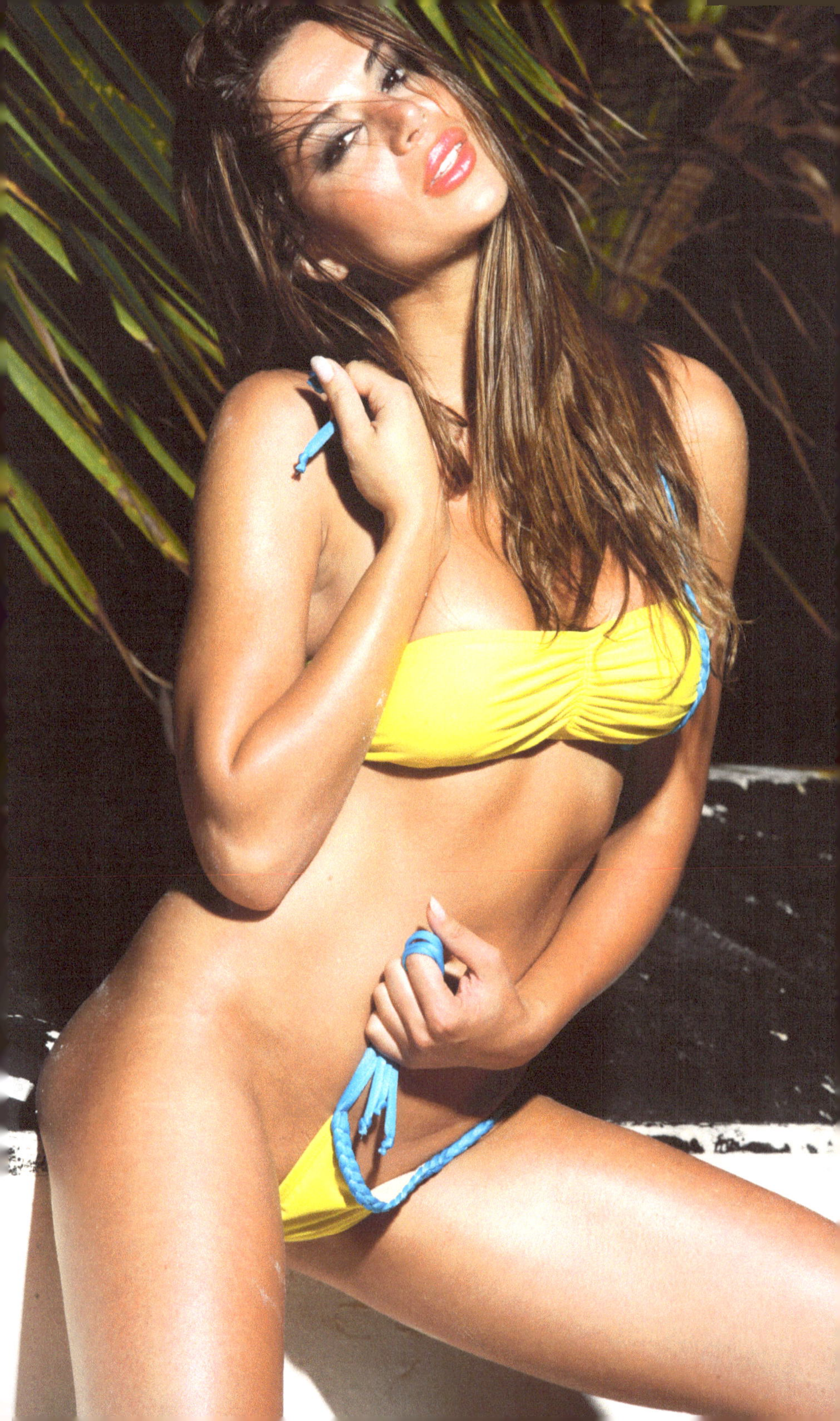

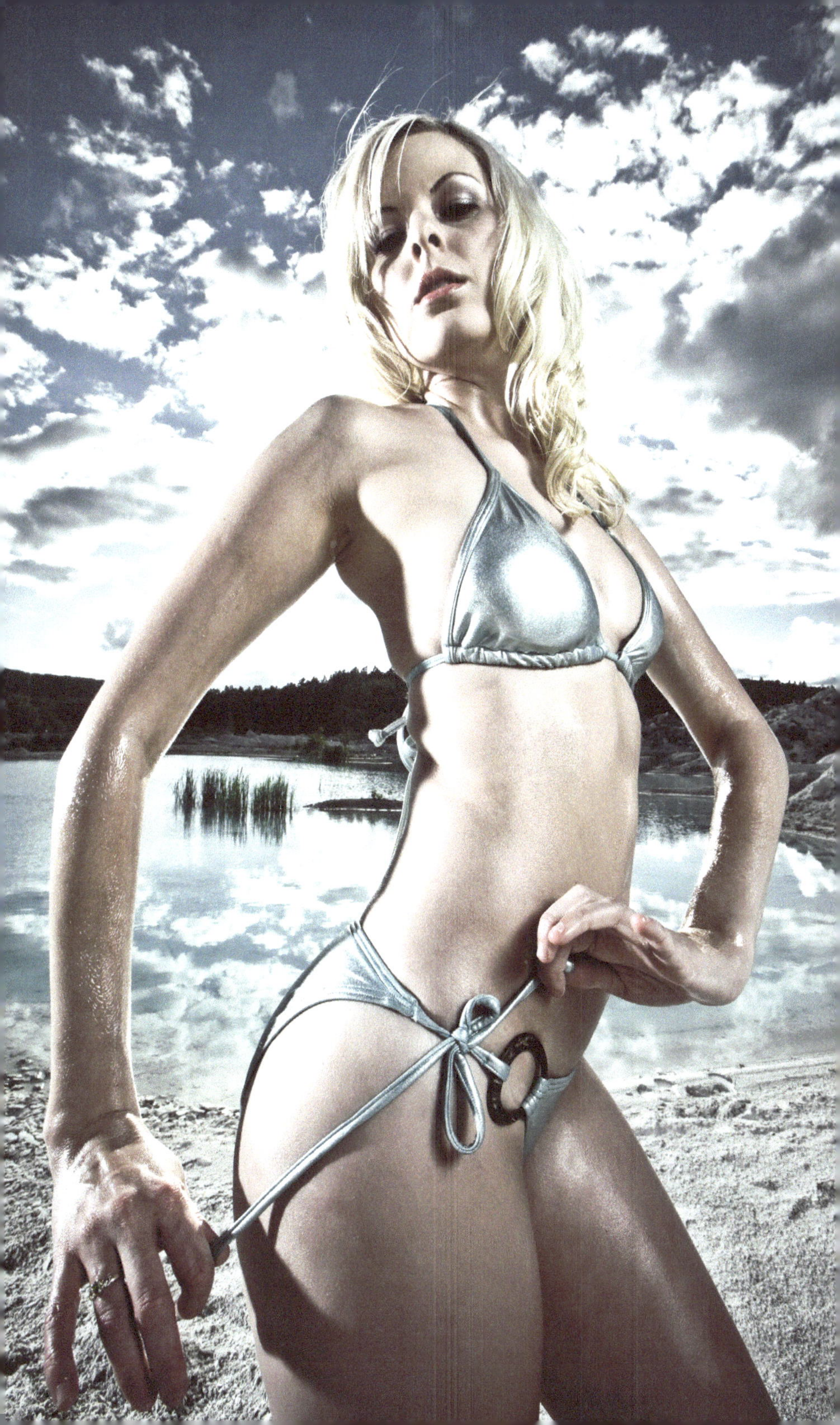

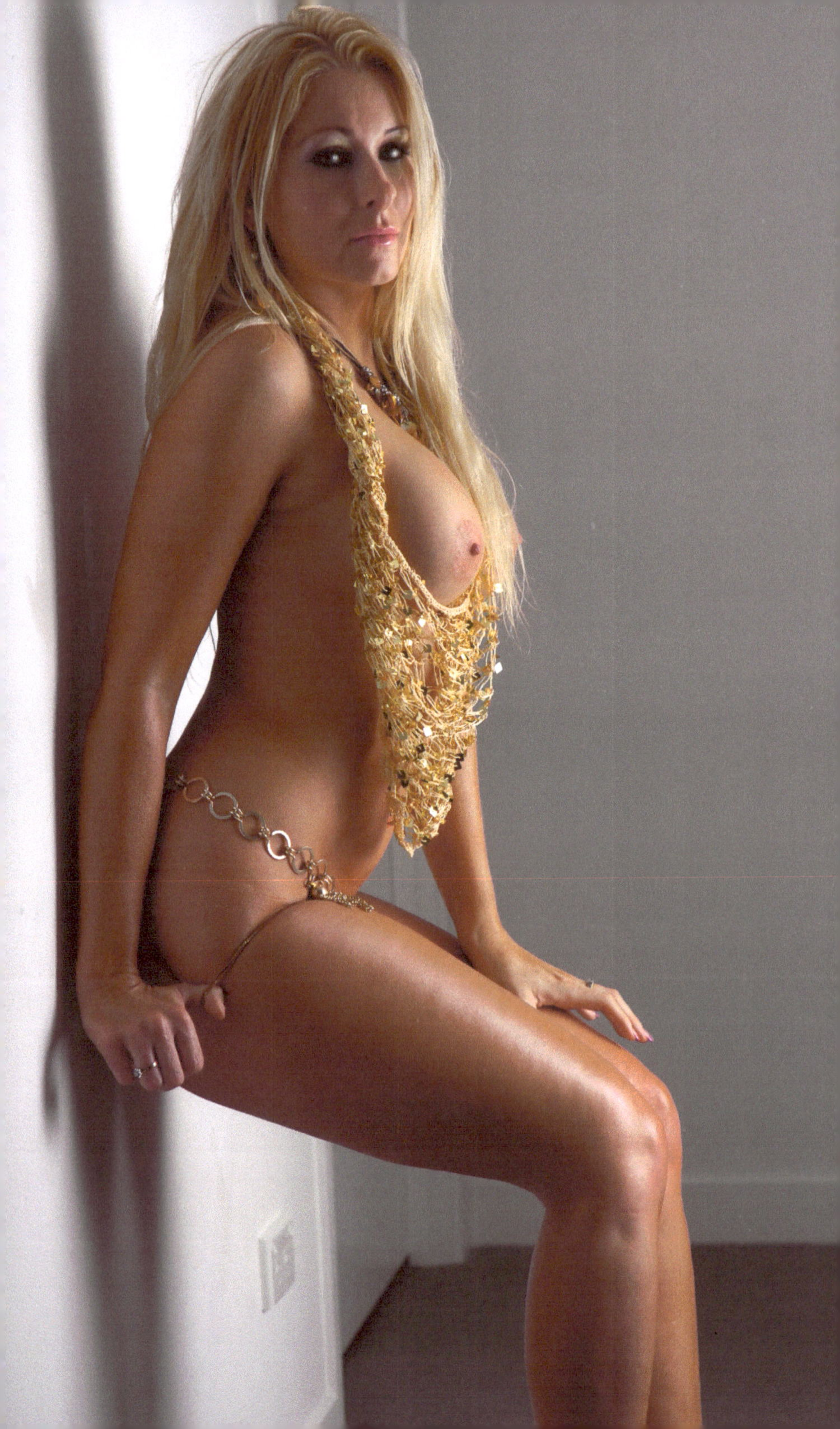

www.ingramcontent.com/pod-product-compliance
Lightning Source LLC
LaVergne TN
LVHW052254100826
845147LV00001B/45

9780986642661